Simple Plane Love

Captain Priyanka Luthra is a trained commercial pilot. After completing her training, she chose to fly small planes to lesser-known exotic places over flying fly-by-wire jets from airport to airport. A dream-chaser by choice, she combined her passion for flying and storytelling in this, her first book. She belongs to the minority community of women pilots in India and now lives in Mumbai.

Simple Plane Love

PRIYANKA LUTHRA

RUPA

Published by
Rupa Publications India Pvt. Ltd 2015
7/16, Ansari Road, Daryaganj
New Delhi 110002

Sales centres:
Allahabad Bengaluru Chennai
Hyderabad Jaipur Kathmandu
Kolkata Mumbai

Copyright © Priyanka Luthra 2015

This is a work of fiction. Names, characters, places and incidents are either the product of the author's imagination or are used fictitiously, and any resemblance to any actual persons, living or dead, events or locales is entirely coincidental.

All rights reserved.
No part of this publication may be reproduced, transmitted, or stored in a retrieval system, in any form or by any means, electronic, mechanical, photocopying, recording or otherwise, without the prior permission of the publisher.

ISBN: 978-81-291-3115-7

First impression 2015
10 9 8 7 6 5 4 3 2 1

The moral right of the author has been asserted.

Typeset by Saanvi Graphics, Noida

Printed at Repro Knowledgecast Limited, Thane

This book is sold subject to the condition that it shall not, by way of trade or otherwise, be lent, resold, hired out, or otherwise circulated, without the publisher's prior consent, in any form of binding or cover other than that in which it is published.

Mom: For teaching me how to walk, run and then letting me fly. You are the wind beneath my wings!

Hemant: For bearing with my unending banter and mostly for just being yourself. You never stop giving me hope!

Mummy, Papa, Aarti, Karan: For the belief you have in me. You guys make it all worth it!

Poo: For the deal we made ages ago. We shall see forever together!

Maneet: For all the conversations; also the silence. May we continue riding on shooting stars!

Harshad: For sharing all the fairy dust with me. You make me believe in magic!

Gagan: For all the reality checks. Please keep them coming!

Contents

Final Call	1
The Pink Pearl	7
Captain G	14
Mayday	20
Grounded	28
Mabuhay	33
Girl Talk	40
The Adventure	47
Magic	53
Taking Chances	60
Serendipity	65
The Surprise	74
The Lighthouse	86

Woman on Top	94
Mother India	105
The Bird and the Fish	113
The Maid of Honour	128
The Fairy Tale	136
A New Day Dawns	148
Sleepless in Manila	158
The Final Approach	168
The Perfect Landing	176
Acknowledgements	187

Final Call

The radio crackled and a familiar voice said, 'Romeo Papa Charlie One Niner Niner Two, exit runway at Bravo, proceed to parking via Zulu Lima.'

Familiar words that I had heard over a thousand times ... so I knew what I had to do, like clockwork. My Commander had already made the mandatory reply call to the tower, while I manoeuvred the aircraft back to where I had taken it out of.

We had just returned to Ninoy Aquino International Airport in Manila; the flight to the island of Cebu and back had taken us four hours. It was an uneventful flight except for a minor bump here and there. That was perfectly normal in this weather.

The aircraft had come to a halt and I made my call: 'Manila tower, this is the final call for Romeo Papa Charlie One Niner Niner Two, this is Captain Meera Khanna signing off for the night.' The voice at the other end responded, 'Roger that, have a good night, madam.'

'I sure hope to have one too!' I thought, as I went through my shut-down checklist. It was part of my duties as a First Officer and I did it every single time, even though I knew it by heart. Captain Garcia, my Commander, about fifty-ish with salt-and-pepper hair and a beer belly, hurried out of the cockpit and walked away. He had been flying charters for about a decade, had ten thousand hours of flying time on the Super King Air C90, the type of aircraft we were flying. He was one of the senior-most guys around. An army of ground personnel boarded to take charge of the aircraft, all talking to each other in Tagalog, a language native to the Philippines, and pausing intermittently to smile at me. Communication was always the bone of contention between me and the locals; they understood English but barely spoke it and I could make out nothing of what they said. They noted the tachometer's readings on their worksheet to calculate the exact flying time, then wrote down the fuel markings from the instrument panel, and handed the worksheet to me so I could sign it. It was over. My last flight in Filipino-land had ended. I picked up my bag and walked out with mixed feelings.

A loader walked towards me, smiled and signalled towards my bag. I was more than happy to hand it over to him. Carrying heavy bags was never my thing! I looked around for my Commander and found him standing at a distance, blowing smoke rings into the air. He looked at me and said, 'So, you are leaving Manila after all; you should have at least stayed for my wedding!'

It was a big deal for Captain Garcia; he was finally getting married to his girlfriend after six years of relationship and two children.

'I wish I could, Captain G,' I murmured with a regretful smile.

We were waiting for the crew transport to take us to the terminal; it was not chilly enough for the first week of December. Being at sea level made the Philippines a very humid place with very mild winters. I got my phone out of the bag. Five missed calls. At least three, I knew for sure, would be from my mother, calling to see if I had landed safely. She did it every single time even though I had been flying for three years now. The phone rang, I glanced at Captain G and said, 'I should take this.' He smiled his best benign smile. 'It must be your mother, go tell her what you tell her every time, sab theek hai, Ma!' he said, in a funny accent.

I laughed as I took the call.

'You hadn't sent me the "landed" message so I thought I'd call.' As always, Ma came directly to the point. I could sense the tension in her voice; it was nothing new for either of us. It had taken her a lot of courage to support my decision to become a pilot. After losing my dad to an air crash she had to fight her fears to let me live my dreams.

'*Sab theek hai, Ma!*' I smiled. 'Just landed, still at the aircraft. Will call you when I am out of here.'

'Don't forget to call like you always do!' She breathed past the relief in her voice.

'I never forget,' I replied. 'Got to go now. Bye, Ma, take care,' I said and hung up.

Talking to my mother always made me smile. I knew she was very proud and very scared at the same time. It was almost a ritual; every time I landed I spoke to her, even if it was just one sentence. It had started with my first flight, and then became a habit.

I walked back to where the crew car was expected to arrive. Captain G had lit his second cigarette by then. I was still looking into my cell phone, trying to figure out who the other missed calls were from. One was from Diana, who stayed in Mumbai. She was my best friend in the whole wide world. The other was an unknown number, thereby making it unimportant for me. Then I called the last dialled number on my list.

'Hello, Em,' said a man's voice.

Adi was one of the very few men in my oestrogen-ruled life. He shifted roles as and when required, from best friend to someone I looked up to. He had been my strength in tough times, as I had been his. 'Shucks,' I exclaimed, 'I woke you up, I am so sorry! It must be about a little past midnight. Go back to sleep, we'll talk in the morning. Okay? Goodnight!'

'Are you done talking? Can I say something, or should I still wait for my turn?' His deep, husky voice flowed down the line, 'How could I be sleeping this early, I was just winding up at work. I was hoping you would call, in fact I was waiting for your call.' It sent a warm, tingly feeling through me. He continued, 'How did you sign off for the night? Did you say "Hasta la Vista baybeh!" like I always tell you to?'

'I am a pilot, Adi, not the Terminator. I ended the way I always do.'

He sighed dramatically. 'You are not that crazy maverick anymore, Meera. You have become so boring.'

'You have no idea,' I mumbled.

'Couldn't get that, say again please,' he said.

'I have made my final call,' I said. 'You go back to sleep now, we'll talk later.'

'If you need me, you know where to find me,' he said and hung up.

It took me a minute to refocus on where I was after Aditya disconnected the call. Talking to him took me away into another space altogether.

I sat in the car that was waiting for me and we drove off to the terminal. I threw a backward glance one more time to see my beautiful companion, RPC 1992, short for its call sign—Romeo Papa Charlie One Niner Niner Two—and blew the aircraft a flying kiss. She stood there in all her glory. Painted red, she had a silver tail. Her perch was elegant as her stride was powerful. 'For all the wonderful times we have had together, standing by each other in not-so-good ones, Godspeed, my love!' I thought as I blew her a flying kiss.

'Did you not name her something?' asked Captain G, smiling from ear to ear at my gesture towards the aircraft.

'Nefertiti! One of the few woman pharaohs in Egypt, also a very beautiful and elegant lady with a chiselled nose, just like our aircraft,' I said in one breath. I was very proud of the name! She was one of my favourite characters in Egyptian history. She was a woman in a man's world, a strong ruler and a loving mother at the same time. A perfect balance!

'I should get that painted on the tail, like they do on war planes,' he said. 'Does that qualify as your farewell gift?' Captain G was giggling now! He had a very funny laugh, which was a lifesaver at times when I did not find his jokes funny. I laughed at how he laughed. It worked for both of us.

We reached the airport terminal, the place that had been home to me for the last two years. It was always in a rampaging state of comfortable chaos, which to someone new looked like bedlam, but I knew from experience that every single person knew exactly what they had to do, and were doing their job well. 'I'll see you tomorrow, kiddo,' said the Commander. 'Jenny and the kids want to say goodbye.'

I was very fond of Captain G's kids; his five-year-old daughter and I had built her doll's house together. I wanted to see them before I left for India. 'Goodnight, sir,' I said, as I walked towards the car waiting for me.

'Remember,' he screamed at me, '*Kumain!*' Meaning, eat. I nodded and waved to him. I was known for my laziness with respect to food. I had conveniently skipped dinner many times on the pretext of being sleepy. He had taken it upon himself to make sure I took care of my health. So he never forgot to remind me to eat. 'I am going to miss him,' I thought and walked towards the crew car that had pulled over at the kerb.

The Pink Pearl

It was almost three in the morning local time when I eventually left the airport. At the wheel of the car was my usual driver—Ding, a peculiar personality. Medium built but hefty and perennially attired in black, he looked like he had walked right out of *Godfather*, the movie. A Bluetooth set was glued to his ear at all times and he wore the darkest of black shades. He had been assigned by the company to drive me around the city when I first arrived in Manila. Ding took his job very seriously and also doubled as an unofficial bodyguard. He understood more English than he could speak.

'Roxas Boulevard is the most beautiful road in the entire city,' I said as we drove down the brightly lit thoroughfare past the coconut trees that swayed gently in the salty sea breeze, welcoming every visitor to the city. I must have said this countless times earlier. Ding nodded.

I felt safe with Ding around; but it's not that there was anything to be scared of. Manila city was considered very safe for women; unlike most metros back home, women here could be seen walking around at any time of day or night without fear. But I had seen a few episodes of drug peddlers killing tourists on Discovery Channel a long time ago, and those images had stayed on my mind!

'You want to stop at regular place, madam? Or you home directly?' asked Ding.

'I think we should stop for a bit,' I replied. 'I will forget all the English I know if I stay here a little longer, you know, Ding!' My tone was teasing. As I had expected, he did not completely understand what I said. So he just nodded. I looked out of the window. The city was aglow with myriad colours. Multicoloured poles with lights on them lined one side of the boulevard. On the other side was an array of fine dining restaurants. This was downtown Manila, a place that never slept.

The car came to a halt. 'I wait here,' said Ding. I got out and the cool sea breeze hit my face. I was standing at the place where I had come at least once every day for the last twelve months, mostly for a run, but at other times just to feel like a part of the city. I loved the sea. Something about Roxas Boulevard made me love this place.

I was used to receiving a few smiles and a few strange looks. Filipinos really liked Indian facial features and mostly the eyes. '*Maganda mata*' they called beautiful eyes. But today it was different; I was being stared at. I realized something was different today—I was in uniform.

The uniform had always had that effect. I was wearing a crisp white shirt with black trousers, and there were the epaulettes with three stripes on my shoulders and a wing on the right side of my chest. Also an integral part of my uniform was a little Indian flag, which I wore right above my heart. The uniform made people look good. I had hardly seen anyone look bad in it. There was a sense of pride in wearing it. No matter which part of the world you were in, it always felt the same.

The attention felt great at first, but you got used to it as time passed. I had been wearing it for three years now; so I was almost oblivious to it.

I looked up at the sky, and saw the moon staring back at me. We had done this often! It was as if I was a part of a love affair between the earth and the moon; the moonlight kissed the earth, making her arch in pleasure, as she melted into the moon's arms, as if this was the only chance they had; the closest they could get to each other for a very long time. The cold wind wafted around me, humming softly like the sound of their breath in unison, soft yet sensual. I walked further still gazing at the moon, wrapped in the mystique of another magical Manila night when I was distracted by something behind me, something dark like a shadow moving slowly.

I turned to see what it was. It was Ding, moving the car forward inch by inch so he could keep me in sight. 'What an anticlimax!' I said aloud and walked back to the car. 'Home now, madam, or food place?' he asked, blissfully unaware how brutally he had killed a beautiful moment.

'Home,' I said.

The Pink Pearl was one of the most majestic buildings in downtown Manila, and looked like a princess decked up in finery when the lights were turned on. The Pink Pearl had forty-five floors. The first twelve were a hotel and the rest were service apartments. It even had an open-air swimming pool on the thirteenth floor. The entrance was an arc-like structure with two lions on either side, mounting guard. The service apartment and a chauffeured car were among the few perks of working with the largest charter company in the country.

Our car stopped under the canopy that covered half the road it was on. A concierge in uniform came rushing to open the door, and was promptly snubbed by Ding, who was already holding my door open. I had told him many times that I could open the door myself, but he insisted on doing it each time. He got my bag out of the trunk and handed it over to the doorman, who was waiting patiently at our side.

'Should I order a medium-sized chicken carbonara at Red Cab Pizza, madam?' Ding then asked me with a serious, unsmiling face.

'Oh dear God, the man knows too much about me!' I thought. But aloud I said, 'No, Ding, thank you. Please go home. I shall call you in the morning when I need the car.' He nodded again, got back behind the wheel and drove off.

'He could pass for one of the Queen's guards easily, if the Queen chooses to try the oriental flavour sometime,' I thought as I walked into the building with the doorman in tow, dragging my bag. He waited until the lift arrived, and then handed the bag to the liftman. '*Magandang umaga, madam,*' said the liftman. 'Good morning to you too, Cruz,' I said. 'They treat me like a queen, I could get used to this. Living any other way would suck so badly,' I thought.

The lift reached the thirty-fourth floor in a minute. I walked out of the lift onto the carpeted corridor, found my keys and opened the door which had 'Captain Meera Khanna' written in black on the golden nameplate. It was a two-room apartment, with windows on both sides. One had the view of the boulevard and then the endless sea, and the other overlooked the city. The windows had pink drapes on them, which barely resisted the sun. Sunlight would light up the room in a pink hue. I had loved the place from the moment I had set eyes on it. It was a fully furnished apartment, with all the modern amenities. The company had leased it for a year and was paying an equivalent of 70,000 Indian rupees as monthly rent.

The bedroom was a girl's dream come true; it had glass-door wardrobes along one entire wall. A queen-sized bed filled up an entire corner of the room, puffed up with super-sized pillows. Next to the bed was a table with my reading light on it. I had to request the housekeeping—yes, Pink Pearl had this too—to get me one; getting up to switch off the light after I was done reading seemed not only supremely redundant to me, it was also the toughest job on earth. Countless were the days when I had dropped off to sleep with the light on.

Just below the reading light was a picture of my mother, Aditya, Diana and me. It had been taken on my last birthday. And sitting right next to it was the only teddy bear I had owned in my entire life. He was a cute-looking fellow with a red tee that said 'Someone at Stanford loves me'. My cousin at Stanford had sent it to me. There was a little aircraft too. 'These are probably the things I would take along in an emergency,' I had once thought, before ruling out the idea as being dramatic. But the thought did bring home to me the fact that they were supremely important to me.

The bathroom was small but very clean, just how I liked it.

The hall had tan-coloured leather couches placed in front of a 42-inch LCD TV on one side, and a bookshelf on the other. It was empty when I had come in, and now there wasn't enough space to house all the books. Some were lying neatly piled on the centre table. On the corner next to the TV was an idol of Krishna that my mother gave me at Mumbai Airport when I was leaving to train as a pilot.

On the far end of the hall were two counters, separating a little area that had been made into the kitchen. This was the part of the house that was used the least, barring a few times making Canton, the Filipino version of India's Maggi or America's Ramen noodles, and more often than not reheating pizza. The refrigerator was filled with all sorts of drinks, fruit juices with exotic names, flavoured iced tea, and various kinds of beers. It was replenished every day by the very efficient housekeeping. There was a dining table for two, along with matching chairs, which was never used of course.

I changed out of my uniform and into my favourite pair of shorts and a black tee. If it were left to me I would make shorts and tee the official gear, and also award the guy who invented shorts a Nobel Prize.

I washed my face scrubbing it hard, but the kohl loved my eyes too much to quit easily. My watch now said 4 a.m. The sun would be up within a couple of hours. 'I must remember to draw the blinds before I sleep,' I thought while turning the light off. I was standing in a totally dark room, looking out at the sea from my window. This was my dream home. I had always wanted one like this, and was determined to have one looking out at the sea in my own country.

This house had been my kingdom since the time I had walked in. I had lived life within its walls and the house had been a silent observer all the time. It had seen me have animated conversations with friends over the phone. It had seen me fight with my mother over odd little things and cry over them later. It had heard my non-stop blabbering with Aditya and also my silence on days when I didn't even want to think aloud.

It had seen me engrossed in flight planning and learning navigation, pulling my hair out trying to explain to the hotel guy that a vegetarian omelette was not only an oxymoron but also had to be without any chicken or bacon.

It had heard my silent prayers on some days, and my loud contagious laughter on the others. It had seen me bravely extinguish a small short-circuit fire. It had seen the little girl in me jump with joy when India won a cricket match, and cry all night on the couch when my dog in Mumbai passed away.

It had seen me walk out for work every day with pride, and cuddle up and sleep like a baby on days I didn't feel like waking up and didn't have to.

Apartment number 3404, The Pink Pearl, Roxas Boulevard, Manila, has been home and will always be one of my fondest memories, I thought aloud as I drifted off into sweet slumber, totally forgetting about drawing the blinds, as usual!

The soft golden early morning sun spread its toasty tentacles all around me, lighting up my room and making it warm. I did not want to wake up; stubbornly I pulled the comforter over my eyes and shut them tight. The sunrays were more adamant than me, seeping right into whatever space they found. They wouldn't give up, and so I had to give in. I peered into my watch to see what time it was. 'It's only seven. Who wakes up this early on a day off!' I mumbled and grumbled as I drew the window blinds.

'Good morning sunshine, I shall see you in a while!' I said as I dived back into bed.

Minutes later my phone buzzed, it was a text message from Captain Garcia: 'Good morning, Captain Sleepyhead, brunch at 11:00 hours at Aristocrat with Jenny, the kids and me. Bring a date.'

'Affirmative on the brunch,' I replied, 'negative on the date, see you there, goodnight.' Then I set an alarm for 10 a.m. and went back to sleep.

Captain G

After completing my training and getting my Commercial Pilot Licence in the US, I had come to Manila to get my Type Rating on the Super King Air C90. Soon after that I was offered a job by Aerofloat Aviation as a first officer on one of their planes used for charter services. I loved the place and the job was lucrative, so I chose to take it up.

The first time I saw Captain Garcia, he was screaming something in a language I didn't know, and to someone I didn't know. All I knew was that he was super furious. His chubby face was all red. This is not how I had imagined meeting the Commander I was supposed to fly with. He looked at me, stopped screaming, and said in a very low voice, 'You do your job, I do mine. Both of us go home happy, *maintindihan?*'

I wordlessly nodded in agreement. I did not get the word he'd used at the end of that sentence. I couldn't even remember it later for me to Google it. It turned out to be one of the most commonly used words by Captain G. It meant: 'Understood?'

Over the last few months he had become one of the few people I looked up to. He did his job perfectly, ate and drank as much as he wanted, whenever he wanted and he laughed a lot; of course, the best thing about him was that he spoke more than I did!

On every flight he told me something new about his country. He told me how the Philippines had been a colony of Spain for hundreds of years. 'The Americans defeated the Spaniards and then took control of our islands; we went from being slaves of one ruler to slaves of another. Nothing changed for us,' he told me grimly during one long flight. 'Then World War II broke out, and soon it reached our capital. The Japanese were tiny, brutal people; the scars of the massacre have been passed down the generations.'

Talking about the history of the country usually made him sad. He would go silent. But nothing could keep him low for long; all I had to do to get him back to his chatty self was talk about his favourite subject: food! 'Captain G, I don't think we will have the time to stop for a meal after we land, we could just refuel and head back, say what?' He would reply, 'You are right, little lady, you get the aircraft refuelled and I shall get myself some sisig!'

Sisig is a spicy and sour Filipino pork specialty. It could pass off as a greasy version of keema, our minced meat. Like most men in the country, Captain G loved his sisig; he could eat it for all the three, four or five meals he had in the day. He tried his level best to make me eat it. He had even pulled rank on me once.

'As your Commander, I command you to eat it.'

'Sir, I cannot eat it in the interest of the safety of the aircraft and the passengers. They won't be able to survive with both pilots incapacitated,' I said, grinning.

Every time he ordered sisig at a restaurant, I would grin. He asked me a million times why I did that, but I had decided against telling him that I had named him 'Kaptaan Garcia

Bin Sisig'! The name made him sound like a character from a Filipino version of the Arabian Nights!

His sense of humor was the highlight of his personality; he could laugh off the greatest of problems, or perhaps even drink them down. There wasn't a sad moment around him, but the minute he entered the cockpit, he would transform into another person. He taught me almost everything I knew about the aircraft we flew. He knew the machine inside out. And he made sure I did too. Every screw, every rivet was accounted for.

Every time I saw him do the pre-flight check, it was like he was saying a prayer. He would touch the fuselage lightly and keep whispering something. 'Were you praying?' I had mustered the courage to ask him once. He hadn't replied. I had never asked him again.

He conducted the pre-flight personally. Even if I had already done it, he would go around doing it once again. I was sure he knew the number of scratches the aircraft had, and also how they got there. He sighed every time he touched the place where we had once had a bird-strike and the paint was a little chipped.

I admired the way he spoke about the aircraft and I listened intently when he did. 'We have a triangle of trust in here,' he had said once, 'you, me and this beauty. We can co-exist and work together flawlessly only if we trust each other completely. My life lies in your hands, yours in mine and all of ours with her.' He kissed the panel in front of us.

'Every beautiful creation is a woman; it's very simple with them, you have to love them with all your heart and they love you back.' I had never heard anyone talk about a machine like he did. I did not know if I agreed with his theory entirely or not, but there was no harm in trying it on for size.

The first thing I did was to name her—somehow, that made things a little personal between the aircraft and me. I kissed Nefertiti's yoke every time we were ready to rotate during take-off. I knew the fuel systems and the engine like the back of my hand. I considered it the anatomy of the aircraft.

I had always had a notion that there must be some kind of story around Captain G; I knew he was very rich but he was also very grounded. I had a feeling that he had seen a lot in life and had therefore learnt many hard lessons. He had once mentioned, 'Ours is one of the richest families in the country. I was born with a silver spoon in my mouth, but had to remove it so I could smoke a cigarette!' He continued, 'I got everything I wanted as a kid, I did not need to work. I chose to fly. It gave me something that is much more important than money: self-respect. Everyone's life is not as dramatic as the poor-dad-rich-dad story, values are independent of that. I had a rich dad, my children do too. My dad taught me a way of life and I teach my children the same.'

Before taking up the assignment in the Philippines I had researched the country online. I read that the institution of family didn't mean for them what it meant in our country. Western ways were very conspicuous in their way of life, but Captain G had changed the way I looked at things. Values didn't have to have a colour or language. What a dad taught his children remained the same across the world.

Filipino society isn't strictly monogamous; every rich and influential man has a wife and more than one girlfriend. I blamed it on the gender ratio of the country. The number of women I saw was way larger than the number of men. But statistically I was wrong. The men just had to travel across country for work.

I had assumed that Captain G was married since he was rich and not so bad to look at (the uniform did a great job of hiding his beer belly). He was very popular with the women too. I had never asked him and he had never told me anything different.

I had met Jennifer at the cafeteria of the Airline Pilots' Association of Philippines. She had seen me wrack my brains trying to make sense of the menu.

'How can I help you?' she asked. I looked up to see a twenty-five-year-old waitress with oriental features smiling at me.

'I need something vegetarian and not complicated to eat,' I answered.

She said, 'You should have Jugaad rice; it is made especially for Indians!'

'What is it, and why is it made for Indians?' I asked, interested.

'Lots of Indian students come here for getting a commercial pilot's license; one of them taught our cook how to make rice with sauce and veggies, and he called it Jugaad. So we serve it to all Indians,' she said in her slightly broken English.

The story whetted my appetite and I wanted to have it. I placed an order and she walked off to the kitchen.

Just then Captain G walked into the cafeteria; he took the chair opposite me.

'This is my favourite place to eat,' he said.

I smiled, too hungry to continue the conversation.

People all around us were having very loud conversations without subtitles. Therefore I chose to block them out and wait for food.

SIMPLE PLANE LOVE   19

'*Ano ang kinuha u kaha mayaba,*' said Jennifer to Captain G. He merely smiled. She walked off.

I asked him, 'Why did you not place your order when she was asking you for it?'

That was the first time I saw his chubby cheeks go red, as he replied, 'She didn't ask me to place an order; she said, "What took you so long?" She is my girlfriend, and the mother of my children. We are supposed to get married this Christmas.'

My mouth was still open in an O of surprise and embarrassment when Jennifer walked back to our table with two plates. One held Jugaad rice, which later became my favourite dish in the whole country and the other held Captain G's all-time favourite dish, sisig! From across the mountain of rice on my plate I stole glances at the soon-to-be Mr and Mrs Bin Sisig having a nice conversation over lunch.

My verdict was out: Captain Joshua Garcia was a good man!

Mayday

The bond that Captain G shared with me was mainly because we had flown together in crazy times, since the company that we were working for was assisting the government in rescue operations around typhoon-affected areas.

Ketsana hit the east of Philippines on 23 September. It started as a tropical storm but was soon upgraded to a Grade II typhoon. On 26 September the president declared a state of calamity. Ketsana stayed a week, caused landslides, floods, and claimed almost five hundred lives before it passed on to the South China Sea.

We hadn't flown for weeks; the weather wasn't conducive for flying. And when we did, the scene beneath was not a sight that anyone would want to see. The devastation was on a mammoth scale. We were to ferry doctors and survivors back to Manila where relief camps had been set up.

I wasn't about to tell my mother about how bad the situation was, but she got it off the news anyway. When questioned, I would answer: 'They are blowing it out of proportion, it's not that bad.' She had no choice but to believe me.

I was trying very hard—and failing miserably—to keep my cool. My heart had taken over; my brain had gone numb seeing the destruction and the deaths. We were carrying passengers who were sick, hungry and in shock. Two doctors flew with us, so that first-aid could be administered on the aircraft itself. The usual chatter and laughter around the office had transformed into an eerie silence. People spoke only when they were spoken to. The air around us was very heavy.

On one of the afternoon flights I noticed on the documents given to me that the doctors weren't flying with us. I waited for Captain G to finish his pre-flight ritual and asked, 'I don't see the doctors on the passenger manifest. Also, on the flight back it says only two souls on board. Aren't we carrying passengers back?'—'souls on board' being the general term for all people on board, passengers and crew.

'We are carrying back a coffin,' said Captain G without looking at me.

I had no idea how to react to that, in the last few days I had seen a lot of suffering, people losing their houses, belongings and everything they called life. But this was the first time that I was going to see death from a few feet away.

Neither of us spoke on the two-hour flight. When we landed, Captain G walked off to talk to the people standing at the terminal, while I walked around the aircraft. I could see the loaders putting the coffin in. I was handed a set of papers. I didn't have the courage to look through them.

We took off, and only after getting our clearances did Captain G finally speak. 'He was a tourist, backpacking in the country; he will be sent back to his family in Australia.' I didn't want to know, I wanted to treat this flight as just another cargo, but it wasn't possible. I was restless throughout the ride and very uncomfortable. It showed on my face.

'Michael really liked to travel, and we are taking him on his last journey, Captain. Take a deep breath and let's do what we do best—fly the aircraft,' he said softly.

It did not help much; it made me think that I was all alone in the country, just like Michael, doing something I loved to do. But I wasn't ready for the end yet. And I didn't think he was either. The thought sent a chill down my spine. It made me feel sick and tears stung the back of my eyelids.

We made a safe landing, and the first thing I did was call Aditya. 'This is horrible, Adi, I don't think I'll be able to do this again—we just flew back a coffin. A coffin in the cabin of my aircraft! I can't begin to explain how upset I was. I think I should just leave, maybe I will leave and come home tomorrow', I must have sounded hysterical. Aditya had been on the receiving end of all my distress calls since we were kids.

'Calm down, Em—tell me everything that happened. Just let it out. We'll talk about you coming back at the end. You don't have to be there if you don't want to be.'

I told him every tiny detail, and by the end of the conversation I felt lighter. Aditya had always been my fall back person. It was so easy for him to put things in perspective for me. He must have a PhD in TLC (tender loving care) by now. He had been doing it since we were kids.

In the days that followed, things got better in the Philippines. The flights were less turbulent, the sun was back. People at work had started getting their cheer back. Grim faces had tiny smiles on them. Captain G and the ground crew were back to their animated conversations. I was back to staring blankly at them as always. Even after spending months in the country I was still left out in the crew jokes cracked in Tagalog.

We were flying to exotic places again. The sights were getting back to being beautiful. However, this literally was the calm before the storm. Within a week of Ketsana passing through the Philippines, storm warnings made a second appearance. This time it was Parma, a super typhoon which was closing in on the coast. On the horizon were huge towering clouds, like demons looking down, lurking just around the corner, waiting to strike.

Mass evacuation of families was in process, ahead of Parma coming in. The Met department had calculated its path, which was through a few of the most heavily inhabited islands in the Philippines. My crew members and I got in a couple of days of hectic flying, while the typhoon gained momentum over the sea. People hadn't recovered completely from the destruction caused by one typhoon and another one was ready to rain down upon them.

All rules were set aside and every aircraft and pilot that could fly, was expected to fly. The flight duty time limitations imposed on us were overlooked since it was an emergency. Thirty thousand families had to be evacuated. We were on a mission. There were people stranded on islands because the rivers were flooding and dams were overflowing. All we did was fly as much as we could, in torrential rain with crazy winds making it all the more difficult.

As part of the rescue measures by my charter company, I was asked to operate a flight to Bacolod with Captain G—the people from the nearby province of Laguna had to be ferried back. We took off hurriedly since we had a small window of flyable weather within which we had to fly those people to safety. 'Fasten your harness, it's going to be a bumpy ride,' said the Commander.

'That is my line, sir.' I smiled, trying to release the pressure by joking about the announcements I made.

There was not much of a conversation after that, because I got busy multitasking between managing a really bumpy aircraft and the nausea created by it. The landing was the worst I had experienced in a long time. The winds had changed direction at the last minute, we could not go around because we were short on time and bad weather was closing in on us. We landed at the far end of the runway, leaving most of it behind. The flight ended in a huge thump.

Before I could recover from the thump and nausea, Captain G gave out the orders: 'You get the passengers boarded, check the manifest, and I shall do the walk around. We don't need to refuel. Let's get back into the air in ten.'

I got to work instantly. There were five names on the manifest—the names and ages of the people boarding the aircraft are listed on a manifest. As they were being led to the aircraft, I called out their names and they answered. Three men and two women boarded and took their seats. Fear was writ large on their faces, their hands tightly clenched as they held on to whatever was left of their lives.

When I got back into the cockpit, Captain G was already there. 'Looks like you saw an *aswang*!' he commented. The fear I had seen on the faces of the passengers reflected on my face too. It was white, like I had seen a ghost. 'Let me tell you my most favourite four words, Captain Meera,' he said as we got the aircraft rolling for take-off. 'This too shall pass.' I was hoping it would, and fast!

Ten minutes into the flight, we were into a storm. Rain lashed at us from all sides, and was deafeningly loud. And suddenly there was a very loud bang on the left of the aircraft, after which everything went silent for a second. The left engine had shut down and Nefertiti was now banking dangerously towards the left. The passengers were screaming. Before I realized it I saw myself flipping open the 'engine failure' checklist. I had done the drill a lot of times during training, but it was still new to me.

'Aviate, Navigate, Investigate, Communicate.' I had learnt them by heart during my pilot-training days.

There was calm on Captain Garcia's face, who until now had been deftly commanding an aircraft that had been obeying him in a most charming manner, but which was now throwing a tantrum. Captain G was calming her down. He leaned into the cockpit's control board and whispered something. While my Commander had taken charge of the first two things on the list, I had already started with the 'Investigate' part. My hands were moving faster than I thought they could. My brain was working, and my eyes were reading. I was multitasking like my life depended on it. Well, it did.

'Make the call,' I heard him say.

I called Bacolod tower on the radio and said, 'Tower, this is Romeo Papa Charlie One Niner Niner Two, we have port engine failure. Turning around now, request straight in for runway 21.' Within seconds, we had our clearance and priority landing. I squawked 7700 on the transponder. This transmitted a coded message to the ATC through radio frequency. We had declared an emergency. Then I switched to the common frequency which was monitored by most towers and airliners. 'Mayday, mayday this is Super King Air C90, 20 nautical miles northwest of Bacolod Airport, seven souls on board. We have an engine failure. We will be landing on Runway 21, Bacolod Airport.'

Before I switched back from the common frequency I heard someone say, '*Maaring diyos sa iyo*,' and then I heard Captain G say, 'Amen!' This was the toughest part of 'Communicate'—letting the passengers know that we have an emergency. But I had to do it.

'Ladies and gentlemen, this is First Officer Meera Khanna. Just to let you know, we are reverting to Bacolod following an engine failure. We will be flying on one engine, which is a routine procedure that we are well-equipped and trained for. You are in safe hands. Please fasten your seatbelts tightly, and remove any sharp objects from your pockets. Thank you.' I shut the PA system and got back to my checklist.

Captain G had already tried to windmill the aircraft, which was a procedure to restart the engine. We were going to do it one more time before we needed to prepare for landing. I saw it on his face before I heard it. The engine had restarted. We were getting full power back. I had the runway in sight. The landing gear had been lowered. We were going to land safely. And we did! Thanks to the ghastly winds however, we flared, bounced a bit before the wheels decided the tarmac was the best place to be.

I got out of the cockpit amidst sounds of clapping and laughter all around. People were saying things loudly and this time I did not need subtitles! I knew they were all thanking God, and were happy that we were all safe. It was then that I realized my left leg hurt so badly due to the impact of the landing that I could hardly take a step. I could not bend my knee. The muscles were tender, and I was in tremendous pain.

Captain G walked towards me after all the passengers were taken to safety. He wiped away a lone tear that had just rolled out of my eye and said gruffly, 'You did well, Captain. I am proud of you, kiddo!' And he ruffled my hair tenderly. Now the tear blithely rolled down my cheek. I tried to think why it was there. I couldn't find a reason. It was just there. The medics examined the knee later and told me that I had ruptured a ligament and I had to rest it.

That night, after narrating the whole scene to Aditya over the phone I had warned him, 'Don't you dare tell Mum a word of what happened!' I told him everything about the engine failure but kept my torn ligament to myself. I didn't want my mother—or Aditya—to take the next flight to Manila!

'I promise I won't, if you tell me who you thought of, or who crossed your mind when the engine stopped,' he quipped. Like every Hindi movie buff he believed that life passed in a flashback in front of your eyes in the near-death moment. And it was then you saw the one you loved the most.

'I didn't see anyone! I was too busy flying the plane, duh!' I snapped. Needless to say it was a reply that he never believed.

Truth be told, I did have visions of my life flash by during that briefly terrifying moment when I thought my end had come. Just that the last frame I saw in my mind's filmstrip was blurred.

Grounded

It had been raining for the past few days, but today looked particularly overcast. To make matters worse, I was grounded. Thanks to the rough landing and the ruptured ligament the doctor had instructed me not to fly for two weeks because I had a Grade 1 sprain. Resting the leg, icing the injury and anti-inflammatory medicines were the only way to cure it.

Gravity sucked! I hated being on the ground, but decided I was going to make the most of this enforced vacation. I wasn't allowed to fly, but, heck, I could still travel by road! I called Diana. 'Dee, I have a fifteen-day vacation coming up, get here on the next flight!'

Since this was a bit unlike me, who went home religiously during every vacation, Dee was surprised. 'Why aren't you coming home if you have a vacation Em, you could meet all of us, Aunty, Adi and me! We could hang out with the gang!'

I couldn't have told her about the injury. She would have freaked out. Dee was the one who had jumped the most when I decided to be a pilot and cried the most when I was leaving the country to train as one. I really wanted her to come over. Fifteen days of being all by myself was scaring me already.

'I am not coming home and that is decided, you can do so many things here. Snorkelling, bungee jumping, going on a safari, trekking to see a volcano, this is an adventure sports paradise,' I said. I cleverly kept mum about my own ability to leap about.'

She loved adventure sports as much as I did, but we even loved doing nothing. Living in Manila had given me the opportunity to experience the best adventures, I wanted Dee to share them too.

'Em, you are crazy, but I love you for that. So let me see what I can do. Have you asked Adi to come too?' she asked.

'Why would I do that? This is an all-girls' vacation, he would have to change gender to fit into my plan!'

'He is going to be so jealous when I tell him and that will make me so happy! I gotta go now! Will talk when I have the plans made—oh, and do send me the documents I need for the visa. Be safe. See you,' she replied and hung up.

Diana and I had known each other for a decade now. She was very similar to me, yet very different. The editor-in-chief of a very successful fashion magazine, she was the definition of femme fatale. Fashion was just the obvious career choice for her; no one knew fashion better than Dee. She was the pretty girl in a beautiful chiffon dress with the perfect shoes and I was the girl in shorts and a tee. But our thoughts were uncannily similar; we liked the same food, the same books and yes, the same boys too! Though that had never been an issue between us, thank God! She was a workaholic by choice, went out when obligated socially. She missed me in Mumbai, as much as I missed having her around in Manila.

Neither of us really remember how and when we became friends. It was like she had always been there for me and I for her. I was so glad that she was coming to Manila. If it hadn't been for my injured leg I'd have been up and dancing!

✈

I still had a few days of being grounded alone till Dee could firm up her plans. I had to figure out something to keep me busy, that would stop me from going crazy from doing nothing. Meanwhile, Dee would need to sort her very hectic schedule to make space for a vacation. But I was glad she was doing it, she needed it more than she thought she did.

It wasn't easy being grounded. I was addicted to flying, hooked from the moment I had first taken off. But what upset me more was that the rescue missions were still on. My injury had happened at a time my services were needed the most. It was just past lunch when I ran out of things to do and picked up my phone to make a call. 'Ding, could you pick me up in an hour from now? I want to go to the Mall of Asia.' I called him because I needed help moving around and no one would do a better job.

'I come, madam, but doctor said you should not walk. Also, weathergirl reported storm coming to downtown,' came his staccato reply.

'A storm? Again? Well, it's okay, I shall just stay in and watch something on TV. Thanks for letting me know, Ding.' I rang off despondently. I checked the weather on my phone. It did look like a storm was approaching. I sat on the bed, turned on my laptop and let Wentworth Miller in *Prison Break* have my complete attention.

✈

It turned dark sooner than usual that evening, and the winds were stronger than expected. I was too zonked out by the painkillers to make any sense of it. I was happily snuggled in bed when I awoke to an unusually loud sound. It took me a minute to realize that it was the wind against my window. The power was out, only the emergency lights were working. I checked my phone to see the time, it showed 03:00 hours. There was no network coverage. So I could not call or use the data services to find out what was happening around me.

The wind just kept getting louder. I got up to check the window; there was this one place where the insulation was a little ripped, and that was making the window shake. I peered out sleepily to see what was happening, but couldn't make out anything. I was confused, woozy and in pain. The effect of the painkillers had worn off.

A feeble knock on my door caught my attention. I limped to open it and saw the Korean woman who lived next door standing there. She seemed petrified. I had seen her strolling with a baby only a couple of times in all the time that I had been staying there. Things like meeting the neighbours and socializing did not appear on my roster.

'Please come,' she said to me in a heavy Korean accent as her hands grabbed my wrists and pulled hesitantly. I grabbed the house keys and walked behind her; she led me into her apartment.

The first thing I noticed about the place was the lack of furniture. She led me into the inner room; it was much quieter there. The windows were clearly better insulated than in my apartment. 'I scared, the rain is a lot. I have a baby; please stay here, Kapitan, with me,' she mumbled.

'I am here.' I touched her palm and sat on the couch across from her bed, where she cradled her baby who was very restless owing to the chaos around us. The duet between the wind and the rain became increasingly intense as the night wore on. Later I found out that we had had winds raging up to 40 kmph that night.

My neighbour and I sat there not saying a word. Both of us far away from our homelands, strangers almost, yet comforting each other somehow. The storm stayed for the next few hours, making its presence felt every minute. My exhausted brain was trying to make an exit plan in case the windows imploded.

'The safest place in the room is under the dining table, if something goes wrong, you get under it, I go out and get help.' I tried to explain to the lady with my hands waving, pointing and gesticulating wildly. I knew she didn't understand a word of what I said, but she understood what she had to do. A few hours passed without incident as I drifted in and out of sleep a couple of times.

The noise was gradually lessening; the show of power seemed to be from coming a friendly match between two powerful entities of nature. The baby was finally asleep and his mother now fear-free. I smiled my goodbyes and walked back to my apartment.

My knee was ready to disown me any minute; it was imperative for me to take the painkillers, but I would have to eat something first, so that my stomach could sustain them. There still was no network on the phone and so I couldn't call for food; not that anybody would have been able to deliver it anyway. The intercom was down too. There was some leftover pizza and fizzed-out cola in the fridge. That was the only option I had left. Food had never tasted better than that slice of cold pizza that I munched that morning.

Mabuhay

It was day three since my break had begun and I was waiting for Dee to confirm her plans when my phone rang. 'How is the sexy captain doing?' His voice never failed to make me smile.

'I am good, as usual, Adi,' I lied smoothly. I kept mum about my ligament tear. 'How's India's most eligible bachelor doing?'

'Don't ask,' he groaned. 'I am having a hell of a time handling Punjabi aunties and their aloo-gobi-making daughters. Mom keeps digging them up!' I was in splits as he continued grumbling before winding to a halt. 'Anyway, I got a text from your best friend saying she's going to Manila for an all-girls' vacation, and to feel free to be jealous. Let her know I am not one bit jealous.'

Dee and Aditya loved to hate each other and as far back as I can recall, behaved like scrappy teenagers whenever they met. Aditya had been dragged along countless times on shopping sprees and chick flicks where he and Dee had bickered happily from beginning to end. 'She is coming over, Adi. I have a fifteen-day vacation, so I invited her over to enjoy the world-famous Filipino hospitality. You could come too, you know,' I teased, 'instead of staying there and burning in a green stew of envy!'

'I can't just get out of here. In case you hadn't noticed, I work for a living. Now get to the important part, quick. Why aren't you flying for fifteen days?' he asked.

I knew I couldn't dodge this one. Aditya should have been in the CIA. How did he suspect something was amiss? 'I ruptured a ligament on my left leg on that flight where the engine failed, and I am grounded,' I mumbled, remembering that I had carefully chosen not to tell him about it.

'And if I may ask, when was Your Highness planning on telling me about this?' Adi was now one stop short of furious.

'I didn't want to worry any of you, and anyway, you are too far away to be of any help. Also I haven't told Ma, so please don't tell her!'

'Have I told you lately just how stupid you are, Meera?' he said, adding vehemently, 'You are incorrigible,' and hung up. I knew I had upset my best friend by concealing my injury from him. I sighed and called Dee to give her a heads-up on the situation with Adi. She good-humouredly griped about Aditya being jealous of her forthcoming trip to Manila and added, 'Tell me something new, Em—he is always pissed, either with you or me. *Sadu kaheen ka*!' She giggled. She had nicknamed Aditya 'Sadu', since he was always Mr Grumpy when either of us did something he disapproved of.

'I know now you want me to call him and make things better. I will do that, okay! Now go back to your Wentworth Miller, I shall see you day after tomorrow.' I did just that. Wentworth Miller was just what I needed. His super brain was the only reason I watched *Prison Break*. I was excited Dee had finally firmed up her plans.

She landed in Manila two days after we had that conversation. I was at the airport to receive her, sitting in the waiting area, with Ding standing right behind me, my own personal bodyguard. It had been a year since Dee and I had met, other than on video chats. Passengers had started coming out of the arrival hall, and there she was! A tall figure in a white top, blue jeans, brown leather jacket and brown boots. There was a certain poise about her that inevitably drew every eye. I wasn't the only one who'd spotted her; there was a group of Japanese gentlemen dressed in crisp suits with their jaws on the floor. Dee was followed by a loader pushing a trolley of Louis Vuitton luggage in her wake. She pointed to her sunglasses and grinned. I grinned back, those aviators were the limited edition Police shades I had gifted her a couple of years ago. 'Crazy woman,' I thought. 'The way she preserves them, she'll end up willing them to a museum. '

'*Mabuhay*, people!' sang Dee as soon as she was in earshot, 'What does a girl have to do to get a hug from her best friend in this country?' She hugged me tight, whispering, 'You have a man in black staring at you.'

I hugged Dee back and told her, 'His name is Ding and he is my driver and bodyguard. I am so glad you came, Dee: you are the most beautiful thing I have seen in so many months!' I glanced at Ding who took the cue and walked towards us. 'Ding, this is Diana, my friend from India; she will be staying with me for a few days.' There was no emotion on his face; I was used to that by now. 'Dee, this is Mr Ding; he drives me around and is in charge of my security here.'

Ding picked up the bags and we started walking. That's when she saw me limp. 'What happened to you, why you are limping? Em, don't just stand there—tell me what is wrong with your leg—did you have an accident? Don't tell me you were riding a bike and fell down! Why the hell are you smiling at me? Why didn't you tell me you were hurt? Is that why you are not flying?' She stopped short, out of breath.

'Dee, please ... breathe!' I gripped her shoulders. 'It's nothing, I will tell you the how, when, what and why of it when we get home; I am just fine.'

As we sat in the car she said, 'Mr Ding, it would be nice if you could teach me how to talk Filipino, I am very interested in learning new languages.'

'Tagalog,' he said in response, without turning to look at her.

She stared at me, surprised at the length of his answer.

'Tagalog is one of the native languages of the Philippines,' I said. 'And Ding is a man of few words, very few words.'

'*Salamat* in advance!' Diana threw at his unresponsive back. She had obviously learnt a few words of the language on the flight. Ding just kept driving; as far as he was concerned the conversation was over!

We drove down Roxas Boulevard and I could see from her face that she liked what she saw. Both of us loved the sea; we had spent hours sitting on Carter Road in Mumbai, discussing dreams and making plans of working towards them. The sea was a witness to most of the important decisions we had made together. It had shared mutely in our career debates and been a silent observer to our fights. We had made confessions to the sea, and sat there and gazed at it through rough times. We had celebrated and rejoiced at victories with the sea as our companion.

'It's so beautiful,' she said. 'The sea always calms me down; also, back home it made me miss you.'

'I missed you too. Wait till you see the view from the apartment. You are never going to want to go back.'

'You know that can't happen,' Dee said wryly, still looking out at the sea as we drove along. 'The only sad part about my super job is that I can't be stationed outside the country. This is a vacation I have been longing to take for a year! The job is great, Em, and I have worked very hard for it.'

'You've made *Femme Fatale* India's top fashion magazine, Dee! I am so proud of you, babe—you did it, followed a dream, and made it a reality. Uncle must be proud of you now!'

She turned and smiled. 'It's never good enough for him, Em. Now he wants me to get married because his friend George's daughter is marrying a guy from Dubai!'

'He is proud and happy, I know it. He just isn't good with words.' I smiled back. 'But now, you are here on vacation, and I have plans, great plans! So fasten your seat belt, we are ready to take off!'

'Aye aye, captain!'

We finally reached the Pink Pearl after catching up along the way on practically everything under the sun. It felt so good to be with Dee.

The concierge walked up as Ding took the luggage out and said, '*Magandang gabi* Captain, should I get the luggage sent to your apartment?'

I smiled and nodded, while Diana tried not to roll her eyes at me. 'You live like royalty here!' she exclaimed. We walked into the building after telling Ding to take the rest of the day off.

'Good evening madam,' the ever-smiling liftman Cruz said to me. 'Your friend come to see you because you got hurt, very nice.'

'Yes, Cruz, she is my best friend Diana,' I said, and Dee smiled at him, turning on her thousand-watt charm.

'Diana is a very beautiful name, just like a princess,' he said, blushing.

We giggled like schoolgirls as soon as we were out of the lift. As we reached my apartment, we found a basket of cupcakes left on the doorstep. There was a note that read: 'Thank you for the other night, Kapitan—Neighbour.'

'Hmmm! Interesting!' said Dee.

'You don't want to know,' I said, 'it's not half as interesting as you think!' But Dee was already distracted by the interior of the apartment. 'Not bad at all, Captain Meera Khanna, quite impressive!' Dee strode in. 'A sea-view apartment, downtown, with an army of people at your beck and call. This is what you had always wanted, and here it is!' She stood at the window, looking out at the sea.

I shut the door after her luggage was delivered. '*Kya peena hai?*' I asked. 'Should I get you some water?'

'Let's stock up on food and booze before we sit down to our talkathon,' she said. 'Get me some crushed ice and two glasses. And please order that damned pizza you keep eating all the time.'

I picked up Ms Baileys. Like many other things our choice of drink was also the same. On one of our drunken escapades in college we had discussed how Baileys Irish Cream was sweet and smooth and the high it produced was soft too, unlike the harder drinks, and so the drink had to be a lady. That night, it had been christened Ms Baileys!

Dee was the star in college while I was the nerd. She enjoyed all the attention showered upon her, but I was happy being away from the spotlight. She was always overly protective of me. I wouldn't always say it, but my fangs were drawn even if Dee's name was mentioned in vain. We connected within minutes of meeting each other, but what kept us going was the craziness that we shared. Another trait that we shared was our hatred for waking up early in the morning. During the exams, she would set three alarms for the wee hours of the morning, so she could wake me up to study, while she went back to bed. Over the years our bond became stronger. She now owned a piece of my heart.

I had everything I needed right there in the room at the moment. My best friend and Ms Baileys on crushed ice! I began by telling her that my cupcake-gifting neighbour wasn't a hot Oriental man, but a simple Korean lady with a small baby. I told her about the storm.

'Sounds terrifying, I'm glad that lady had you here,' said Dee as we sat nursing our Baileys, looking out to the sea, the wind blowing into our faces from the partially open window. Life was perfect!

Over the next half hour, I poured out all my pent-up tension. I told her about the engine-failure incident and how I was terrified and yet ended up doing my job. I talked about how it seemed like Captain G had some supernatural powers at that moment. I told her how that incident had changed me, how the pain in my knee only reminded me to be thankful to be alive. Dee leaned back on the sofa and stared at the bluish-grey vapour churning above the sea, myriad emotions dancing across her face. She hadn't said a word since I had started talking about the crash. When I stopped talking she raised her glass and said, 'Cheers to you, Em, and *mabuhay* Captain Meera!'

Mabuhay was a salutation which meant 'long live' and was used to show respect. She always made me feel like a star, and she had done it once again! 'Cheers to us!' I raised my glass too. 'And to a wonderful time in Pinoy land from tomorrow.'

Girl Talk

The next morning I shot out of bed to the incessant ringing of the intercom. It was Ding, on time as usual, but just this one time I wasn't ready, as I normally would be when I had a flight scheduled. 'We'll be there in thirty minutes, Ding,' I said, trying to sound as awake as I possibly could, 'you can have breakfast in the meantime.'

'I wait at the car, madam,' he said. I hung up and awoke Dee hurriedly. '*Uth jaa yaar, woh Ding bhaisahab already on duty hain!*' I continued, 'We must be ready, packed and downstairs in thirty minutes flat, samjhi madam?'

'Wake me up when you are dressed with fifteen minutes to go,' she muttered groggily. I was used to Dee's ways; she would wake up right at the last minute and still be on time. So I packed, got dressed slowly owing to the leg and waited, and magically she was ready almost at the same time as me. 'I am just carrying all my bags, you never know what you need when,' she chirped brightly.

Knowing Dee's fetish for shoes, I was sure one of those two big bags contained only shoes. Back in Mumbai, we had stopped counting the number of shoes she owned, after she hit a hundred pairs. I didn't have a problem with her buying shoes; my problem was they didn't fit me! They were two sizes too big.

We reached the car when Ding was done loading all the bags. I had entered the coordinates of Subic Bay into the GPS. It was about 130 km from Manila. The roads ranged between the best freeway in the country to a single lane mud path. Both of us loved the roads without discrimination.

As soon as we sat in the car, my phone rang. 'Hello Captain, all set for the road trip?' asked Captain G. Intuitively he sensed my nod of assent and went on with his fatherly advice, 'Don't stress your leg unduly if you plan on flying in the near future, and also make good use of Ding. He knows the place very well; that is one reason I suggested you go there.'

'Yes, sir,' I said.

'Also, the place you are booked at is on top of a mountain; so even if the worst weather scenario reoccurs you will be safe.'

'Thank you, Captain G, you are the best,' I told him.

'I know that, you take care now,' he said and hung up. Dee was talking to someone on the phone too, and it looked like she was issuing some instructions at work. I remembered I hadn't spoken to my mom at all in the last twenty-four hours. So I called her. 'Hi, Ma! *Kaise ho aap*?' I said.

'I am good; I knew you would get so happy and busy with Diana that you wouldn't get time to call your only mother,' she joked and then asked, 'Did she give you the stuff I sent for you, does the top fit you?'

'Hanji Ma, I got it, the top fits me just fine, thank you,' I said. 'Now I have to go, we are leaving in a minute!'

'Take care, both of you,' she said.

'Yes, Mom! I love you, bye,' I said and hung up.

Half an hour later, we were finally on the road, the wind whipping our hair. Dee, who was still annoyingly on her Blackberry, finished her office calls and asked me, 'Did you call Sadu?'

I shook my head.

'Lemme call him.' She was already on it. 'Hello! Sadu? Wassup! Em and I have just begun our road trip; now tell me how jealous are you?' She was smiling. 'Oh c'mon now, Aditya, I know you are jealous, you are horrible at lying, haven't I told you this before? You should quit trying. Yeah, yeah, now before you go all Aditya on me, I am handing the phone to Em ... of course we will have fun, of course!' she said as she handed the phone to me.

'Dude, she just won't give up!' he said to me.

'*Tum dono bilkul pagal ho!*' I giggled. My friends were mad!

'I know,' Aditya added, 'I don't have to remind you to have fun, and also be responsible. You know all that. So I am only going to say don't miss me too much!'

'Hmm! We'll try and remember that, talk to you later, Adi. Bye!'

'Bye,' he said and we hung up.

Dee was looking at me funnily. 'Only bye? No "I love you, miss you baby"?' she asked.

'Have you freakin' lost your mind, Dee? Adi and I are great friends and just that!' I retorted. To tell the truth I had given a lot of thought to what Aditya meant to me, and the answer was always ambiguous, confusing and a blur.

Dee tossed back her silky hair. 'I am glad you said that, I don't believe in the concept of love anyway. Very overrated and confusing. 'It's supposed to make you very happy, but some of the saddest people I have ever met blame love for their misery. Weird, no?'

I had always known this about Dee—that she did not believe in love. She had once, in college, loved someone very dearly. He had left her with a shattered heart, broken promises and scars that reminded her of the pain she went through. We never spoke about it, but it had changed Dee forever. She was so focused on her career and what she wanted to do with her life that she had no time for love. She was also very vocal about it. 'How can someone say falling in love is a good thing Em? It's the one thing I can never imagine myself doing.'

I decided to step in to save love from being completely decimated, but had to fall back on theory. 'If I were to believe all the books I've read, it just happens to you and changes your life forever. It's beautiful and magical, serene and divine. It's pure and makes you feel like the luckiest person on earth— that's what the books say,' I added hastily as the expression on her face stopped me in my tracks.

'You have to stop reading those soppy romance novels, they are affecting your brain,' she said, still looking astounded. Then she warmed up again. 'Tell me, if love is so profound and happens to everyone, why hasn't it happened to you, or me? Why haven't we been swept off our feet and carried away into wherever?'

'I think it hasn't happened to us,' I replied cautiously but truthfully, 'because we haven't given it a chance. We are too busy making other plans with life. You have to give love a chance, Dee, a chance to prove its worth, one chance to show you what it feels like to be in love.'

She looked at me, gave me a tap on my head and said, '*Tu pagal hai*', and just when I thought I had made a point she broke the spell of my magical words by asking Ding if he had ever been in love.

'Yes, Po,' he answered, which surprised me enough to make my head swivel in his direction. 'I fell in love when I was in school, with a girl in my class. Now I am married and have four children,' he continued.

'What happened to the girl?' Dee asked.

'She also married now,' he replied.

We exchanged looks, and I said, 'How sad!'

'Why sad, madam? I am happy,' said Ding.

'You are happy that she is married?' Dee was now very interested.

'Yes, Po, I am happy she is married now, and has my children,' he answered.

This was the first time Ding was having a conversation with anyone to my knowledge. He seemed to be very interested in the discussion about love! And Dee was enjoying it even more, because it seemed like he was on her side. 'She has your children?' Dee exclaimed. '*Ajeeb baat hai*,' she said to me.

'Yes, she has my children, and I still love her like I did when we were in school.' Ding was smiling, or at least I thought he was.

And finally it struck both of us dimwits at the same time. 'You are married to her!'

'Yes, Po, I married her when we finished school. My father told me if you meet a good girl marry her before she becomes bad. So I did. Now we are happy.'

'And now your dear Captain madam is going to go "awww" on both of us,' Dee said wryly, but Ding had quit the conversation just as abruptly as he had leaped in.

'I like love stories, and more so the ones which end with "and they lived happily ever after"; what is so wrong in that, Dee?' I frowned.

'There is nothing wrong with it, sweetie; fiction is good until you remember it is fiction and not reality. I have seen so many girls waste their lives waiting for the knight in shining armour, and then lose heart when he doesn't come,' she said, 'or worse, when he does sweep her off her feet and then she discovers his feet of clay!'

'I am not waiting for anyone to come, but I won't mind if he did stop by.' I giggled.

She smirked. 'I don't have the time or the inclination for the knight in shining armour. There is enough love going around me, I love my work, I love you and my family, I have no more to give away.' She was adamant. 'Also, if the damn knight had to come, he would be here already!'

'He is probably just lost, Dee—you know men and their problem with asking for directions! Or maybe he just can't locate your GPS coordinates, you are such a high flier after all,' I suggested hopefully.

'Can we just talk about something else, I am bored.' She faked a yawn. 'Tell me where are we going and what we are going to do there.'

There was no point pushing it since she wasn't interested, so I told her we were going to Subic Bay, which was a naval base, and a haven for adventure sports. We were going to see shipwrecks and fly around in training aircraft. Captain G knew someone who owned a flight training school in that area and who had been generous enough to accommodate us. We were also going for a safari.

'Tell me about what I want to hear,' she said.

'Yes, ma'am, it is a shopper's paradise. It's a duty-free port, so you can indulge to your heart's content and so will I!' I said and she was smiling again.

It was a four-hour drive, and both of us needed to catch up on the sleep we had sacrificed to girl-talk the night away. So Dee and I slid off to opposite corners of the seat and made ourselves comfortable. I had almost dozed off when I heard Diana say, 'Good night, Mr Ding.'

And he replied, '*Magandang gabi, Po.*'

The last thought I remember having was, 'Dee can even get statues to talk.'

The Adventure

I woke up uncomfortably, my neck angled oddly against the backrest of the seat of Ding's car. When I looked outside it seemed like another world. We were in a place which looked like a village. The roads weren't great. The houses were small. People were dressed differently. It was like we were in the middle of a jungle. I looked at my watch, we had been travelling for over two hours, but this place looked like we had gone back in time. 'Where are we?' I asked Ding.

'Lubao, madam. We just got off the highway, for a little time no good roads,' he replied. I looked at Dee who was still fast asleep. She so deserved this vacation. She had made work her life. I was glad she was here. Letting her hair down was something she needed to do more often. After two more hours on the bumpy roads, two Starbucks Frappuccinos and over a hundred pages of Richard Bach's *Illusions*, we reached a city.

'This is Olangapo, madam,' Ding said with a hint of flourish in his otherwise neutral voice, 'this is the last city before we enter Subic Bay; this is like Filipino version of Vegas!' It seemed to me that our man liked this place. 'You have everything here, strip clubs, all-night casinos, anything and everything you like.' I shook Dee, she woke up and stared blankly at me. 'Are we there yet, Captain?' She stretched her arms and yawned.

'We are in mini Vegas, the last city before we enter the bay area!' I said.

The people were dressed in very loud garish clothes, the women in extremely short shorts and tight tees and the men in loose football tees and long shorts. It was a South-east Asian version of how they saw the US. There were pawn shops on the main road, delis, salons and a mall too. There were people on the side of the road selling CDs in stalls. There was English pop music blaring intermittently. This was another world. Just four hours into our adventure, we had seen three very different parts of the same country.

We were stopped by guards at a barricade. They asked for our IDs and wrote down our passport numbers. I noticed that even the locals were wearing some kind of passes. 'What is happening here?' I asked Ding after we crossed the guards. 'We just enter Subic Bay, madam, place has restricted entry. Not everyone allow to enter. This was American naval base, now it port, merchant ships and naval ships dock. It is exclusive place, you will see,' he assured us.

Subic Bay was the opposite of the area we had just crossed. The roads were broad and extremely clean. The hedges rimming the roads were neatly trimmed, there were people working by the wayside, wearing uniforms. The locals were dressed differently; this was almost similar to Manila but with a more international crowd. And then we saw the sea. 'That is such a beautiful sight, the sea at the foot of a mountain!' exclaimed Dee.

'Look at that runway, Dee, set atop that cliff. It almost completely overhangs the sea. And that ship, I think it's an oil tanker...it's huge!' Not that my Dee would ever get excited over a runway that guaranteed a hairy touchdown, or admire a massive ship. Even as I spoke she had turned and was beaming at all the shops. I shook my head.

'There is a Guess, and I see a Gucci too. Oh wait, there is an Aldo there as well, I am sure there are many more... and this is a duty-free zone! Babe, those gates we just entered through are the gates to heaven!' she said with gleaming eyes. This place was perfect for both of us! Captain G had been very thoughtful while suggesting it. I made a mental note to buy him a thank you present.

We were now driving uphill. On both sides of the curvy road was a dense forest burgeoning with trees I had seen only in this part of the world. A few miles into the drive we saw a board which said 'Jungle Safari'. Dee patted my knee. 'Happy little girl, aren't you now!' she joked.

'See what I was talking about! And I am not going in there all by myself!' I said.

'I am carrying my trekking boots and jungle wear, so I am game!' She smiled back. We kept going higher and deeper in the jungle. 'Are we going to stay in a machan?' Dee questioned. 'I had checked out the hotel online; it was huge, like a castle! I even checked out the loo! Didn't look like a machan at all.'

I said 'No,' looking confused.

'Are we lost, Mr Ding?' Dee asked. He just shook his head.

'*Yeh jawab kyun nahi deta yaar, baat karne se paise kaat lete ho kya?*' Dee looked at me obliquely, wanting to know if I cut his pay if he talked.

'*Woh keh raha hai nahi, to nahi hoga. Is jagah ko achhe se jaanta hai who. Tu chill kar na yaar,*' I said, telling her to chill, because if Ding had said no, that meant we were not lost. He knew this place very well.

'I don't care if we have to stay in a freaking tree house, babe! Just that the loo should be clean and usable,' she said, I just nodded. A few more miles and lots of ascending turns later we reached what looked like the top of the mountain. Houses with sloping roofs peeped out of the dense habitat. Then we crossed something that looked like the local marketplace—a couple of shops and one restaurant. 'This looks like a ghost town, I see no people here!' Dee said.

'This is going to be one hell of an adventure!' I replied.

And then suddenly, we were there! A majestic white building loomed in front of us, hidden until a moment ago behind a thick curtain of green. The name on the arched entranceway read 'The Mirage'. That put a smile back on our faces. The place still looked deserted though. 'This is the hotel, madam,' Ding finally spoke.

'So I see,' I said. 'You talk to reception, I get bags,' saying this, Ding went to the car. We walked to the reception. The beauty of the place was surprising, the old-style interiors hid modern decor that elegantly blended in. A man in uniform, possibly the porter, smiled at us and rushed outside to help Ding with the bags. The girl behind the reception desk smiled a wide smile of welcome. 'Good afternoon, ladies!'

'Good afternoon, we have a reservation with you,' I replied, 'it's in the name of Captain Meera Khanna.'

'Yes ma'am, we were expecting you,' she said while handing me a form to fill, 'your room is ready; it is the one that overlooks the valley and also has a sea view,' she added.

'Are there any other people staying here, or is it just us?' Dee interjected. The girl smiled. 'We have fifteen rooms in all, ma'am, and all of them are booked, some of them for months at a time.' I finished filling the form and gave it back to her. 'Months?' I asked.

'Yes ma'am, people come here to relax, mostly international travellers. We have the best relaxation treatments available in the whole country; you can make use of them too. There are meditation sessions every morning, and yoga all day. There is a list of activities available in your room.' Smiling, she added, 'Some people also come for adventure, the jungle safari, the ships and the planes.'

'Well, thank you for all that information,' Dee said, 'you might have to make another category after we leave, the people who come to shop!' Ding walked in with the porter and the luggage. 'Will you be staying somewhere close by?' I asked Ding. His expenses on an official trip would be covered by the company. But Ding needed no such help. 'My wife and children stay in Olangapo, the city outside the gate,' he replied. 'Take me thirty minutes to get here, when you call.'

'I don't think we will need you, Ding. You can enjoy your time at home while we are here,' I said. 'The hotel is providing us with a car and a driver, who will be available all the time.' That was all too complicated for Ding. He looked at me blankly.

Dee stepped in. 'Just go Mr Ding. I shall take good care of your Captain madam and I promise to keep her out of trouble.'

I added, 'We can call you anytime, don't worry. Just go and spend some quality time with your family.'

'No vacation from company,' said Ding sadly.

'I will tell Captain G and no one else needs to know; now go, Ding!' I told him.

'Thank you, madam,' he said. 'My wife very happy!'

'Just one more thing,' Dee said to Ding who was now walking towards the door, 'smile, Mr Ding! That will make us very happy.' I hit her on the shoulder.

'I will,' Ding replied and this time we definitely saw him smile!

✈

Ours was a fairly large room with a glass wall at one end, with Victorian drapes. The porter set our bags down and drew back the curtains. The view left us breathless. A few feet from our room was the valley and then the vastness of the sea unending till the horizon. We just stood there a moment, soaking in the scene. 'I think we should get something to eat,' Dee said, without looking at me. Her eyes were still glued to the view.

'Hmm, I'll change and then we can go out,' I replied, still under the spell of what I saw before me.

'Hey Em, I am glad you are here sharing this moment with me, 'cause I don't think I would want anyone else here except you. Thank you for being…well, you!'

'Hey Dee,' I replied, '*senti mat ho yaar!*' and I stuck my tongue out like we used to when we were kids. 'Get dressed or I am going without you,' she said, making a return-face at me. I was loving every minute of her being there with me. On the way out of our room, we saw a tall good-looking man in cargos, bare-chested, carrying a surf board and walking towards us. As we crossed paths he smiled and said, 'Hi!'

I smiled back and nudged at an already beaming Dee. 'Hi,' she said and we walked on. As soon as he was out of earshot Diana took out her aviators, popped them on, turned to me and smiled. 'Let the adventure begin,' she said and we burst into uncontrollable giggles.

Magic

We decided to take a tour of the whole city before drawing up a list of all the things we wanted to do and see during our stay. The driver was a very friendly chap, trained in the subtle art of entertaining tourists. He had grown up in the area and knew it like the back of his hand. Soon after we pulled out of the hotel parking lot he stopped the car, pointed in the direction of a bunch of tall trees and said, 'That is Bat Stop. If you ever get lost in the area, ask directions for Bat Stop, the hotel is straight from here.'

I nodded, having gathered the reason for the name, but Dee had to ask, 'Why Bat Stop? Are these trees used to make cricket bats?'

'No, madam,' said the guide patiently, 'look up, there are hundreds of bats hanging upside-down from the branches. So it is called Bat Stop.'

Dee shrieked, 'We are never venturing out alone here, Meera. Are you listening to me?'

As we descended from the mountain, the driver—whose name we learnt was Elijah—explained the lay of the land: the marketplace, the community centre, the church, the places where we should not venture alone in the dark and so on.

We told him we wanted to eat something local and wanted recommendations for a good place; so he took us to his favourite place on the mountain top, a hot dog stand!

I saw an old man in vest and shorts sitting at one of the tables facing the valley. He had unkempt hair and a long white beard. On his table was a glass of cheap whisky with the bottle standing next to it. He looked more a Westerner than a local, but he blended in perfectly. He had a pen and a book and was writing, when Elijah walked up to him and shook his hand. 'Captain! This madam is also a captain, only she flies planes,' he said, gesturing towards me.

'Hello sir,' I said as I walked up to him.

'Hello!' He looked at me and said, 'Where have you come from, sweetheart?'

'We are from India, sir,' I replied. By this time Dee had walked towards us too. 'And what brings two pretty girls so far away from civilization to this lonely peak?' he asked laconically.

'We are here on a vacation, the place is so beautiful...!' Dee replied.

'This place is magical.' He nodded. 'There is magic happening all around, you just have to see it.'

We got our hot dogs, waved him goodbye and sat in the car. 'He has been here for fifteen years, madam,' Elijah informed us. 'He was the captain of an American navy ship when Subic used to be their naval base; he got posted here and never left.'

'How does he live, as in, where does he get the money from?' I asked.

'He gets a pension every month, in dollars, and he spends it here in pesos, so he never runs out of money!' Elijah grinned.

'Why did he not leave, Elijah?' Dee asked.

'He fell in love with a girl here, madam, her name was Carol. He stayed back for her. They never got married, but they loved each other so much that he didn't go back even when she died.' For a minute none of us spoke.

'He says he still feels her presence around him, and so he can't abandon her here, to be all alone. Some people say he has lost his mind with grief and has gone completely mad, but other people say that his love is so pure and true that it has broken the boundaries of life and death,' concluded Elijah.

That sentence gave me goosebumps. I had always thought love like that existed, but had never seen it up close. 'What a touching story, and what an amazing love. He seemed pretty sane to me.' I looked at Dee for confirmation. She just smiled; for once, she was lost for words.

We soon reached the mall in the centre of the bay area. I knew it was going to be a long evening with Dee's shopping mania, so I suggested we grab a coffee before we started. Unlike at the peak, there were quite a few people around here: some tourists and a lot of locals.

'You know, the good thing with us here is that no one knows Hindi!' Dee giggled. 'We can say whatever we want to and no one but you and I will understand!'

I nodded in gleeful agreement. We spotted a Starbucks and walked towards it. I noticed a lot of men around who in navy whites. 'Some ship must have just docked, there are a lot of sailors around,' I said.

'Yes, I see hotties in uniform all around us. You know, people say a sailor has a girlfriend at every port!' said Dee dreamily.

'They say that about pilots too, but it's not one bit true!' I retorted.

'You can't manage one "good friend"; so you have no chance of having multitudes, I know!' She was laughing now while we stood in line to get our coffee.

'I am going to the washroom, get me a tall latte and a muffin,' I said, as I stomped off in a huff.

'*Meera, yaar gussa mat ho, aur yahan ki stupid currency to samjha de mujhe!*' wailed Dee as she struggled to make sense of the local currency. She was still standing in line when I got back, and just behind her stood a smart-looking guy in naval whites.

I went and occupied a corner table close to where Dee stood in the queue. Dee turned, saw me and beckoned. '*Idhar aa, Em.*' She waved some notes, saying she would end up paying a thousand instead of a hundred, '*Dekh wo sau rupay mangega main hazaar de doongi, mehengi padegi yeh coffee tujhe.* Serves you right, if this is the most expensive coffee you ever have.'

The man behind her had turned away to talk to somebody, and I grabbed the opportunity to show Dee with a quick glance in his direction that there was something interesting behind her. Turning her neck delicately and getting an eyeful of the man behind her in dazzling whites, she frowned at me and mouthed, 'Behave yourself,' after which she ordered muffins and a latte, opened the wallet I had left with her and took out a bunch of notes. I got up to walk towards her when I heard a deep male voice say, '*Aap dollars bhi de sakti hain, mohtarma.*'

Dee froze. 'I...I can pay in dollars, you say?' she stammered, as he smiled and walked past her, telling the boy at the counter, 'Please add an "Americano Grande" to the lady's order,' and paid for the whole lot as Dee stood stupefied. Now that was unexpected, I thought. This guy had surprised me and flummoxed my unflappable Dee.

'*Aapki table tak pohoncha dun coffee?*' he said, asking Dee if he could get our coffees delivered to our table.

'You didn't have to do that,' she said, referring to his paying our bill.

'Right! But now that I have, you can treat me some other time.' He smiled. I walked up to them. 'Hi, thanks for that,' I said, adding, 'we didn't think anybody here would understand Hindi!' He smiled at that and then, turning to Dee, said, '*Yahan ki currency hai hi itni confusing, saare note ek jaise dikhte hain.* Isliye I prefer using dollars.'

Dee nodded; the local currency notes did indeed all look the same. 'Thanks again!' she said. 'Why don't you join us, now that you have bought the coffee and all?'

'Thanks,' he said, walking slightly ahead of us toward our table. I tapped Dee on her shoulder and whispered, 'Be nice, I like him.'

'I am Diana,' said Dee to Navy Whites, 'and she is Captain Meera. Not the water kinda captain, the air kinda captain.' I just couldn't stop laughing.

'I got that, we don't have women captaining a ship with the merchant navy, even now,' he said.

'Is this your first time docking here?' I asked.

'I have come here before, it's a fairly common route. We stop here for a week every time we pass by. I love being here, the peace, the beauty and the simplicity of life here makes me fall in love with the place every single time,' he said. 'Have you ladies come here for the first time?'

'We just drove in a few hours ago,' Dee said. 'Meera is based in Manila, and I am visiting her.'

'Oh great! One hour ashore and I am already crashing an all-girls' vacation. Lucky me!' he said.

'Don't flatter yourself,' pat came Dee's reply even before I could blink.

'You are too pretty to be so angry all the time,' he said to Dee.

'I am not always angry,' she said without smiling.

'You could have fooled me,' he muttered under his breath. I didn't want to interrupt the conversation or the sparks that were electrifying the air, so I just looked into the coffee mug that was in my hand and pretended I wasn't there. 'Also I am not used to getting compliments,' Dee was saying now on a placatory note.

'Do you work with blind people?' he asked, 'because there is no other plausible explanation why anyone wouldn't tell you how pretty you are!'

'Thank you.' Dee smiled at last and it was like the sun coming out from behind the clouds. I could see even he was taken by surprise as he blinked stupidly. 'Now please stop before I walk off,' Dee said.

'So typically Dee,' I thought. 'She just won't cut him any slack. Not even for a moment.'

'So tell us, Captain, do you have a girlfriend in every port?' I asked, and so the topic changed.

'I am not a ladies' man, Captain. I plan to be just one lady's man, whenever that happens,' he replied.

'Unusual for a sailor,' Dee commented.

'Unusual is my middle name, ma'am,' he said, flashing a winning smile. I looked at Dee. She was impressed; it was just that she wasn't admitting it yet! I, on the other hand, was enjoying the fireworks! 'How do you like the place, Captain?' he asked me.

'I think it is magical,' I replied and winked at Dee, 'a place that can make you fall in love.' Dee smiled back at me with a look that promised me hell later! The thing that struck me most about him was that he hadn't seemed desperate to talk to us. He wasn't trying too hard. That had always been an instant hit with me. Maybe this place is truly magical, I thought. Maybe the magic would work on Dee and fill the void in her life and make her happy! I liked that thought.

Taking Chances

We finished the coffee, said goodbye to Navy Whites, whose name we had still not asked, and then headed for the Guess store in the mall. 'Look at that bag, babe, I think I should get it for your mom!' Dee exclaimed.

'I like it, but I am not sure Mom will,' I replied doubtfully.

'I'm buying it anyway, if she doesn't like it...I will! Ha ha!'

'We'll have to buy a house for the shoes and bags that you keep buying,' I responded. We shopped like there was no tomorrow. I bought red shoes, and then because I didn't think I had a red dress to go with the shoes, I got a red dress, and then a belt, just in case I needed one with jeans. Dee bought two bags and a dress, a belt for her dad and shoes for her cousin. By the time we paid up, Elijah had brought the car around and we drove back towards the hotel. It was time to act on the second thing on our to-do list. Eat good food! Once in our room, we plonked ourselves on the bed and ordered a big dinner from room service. We weren't big eaters, but we loved the variety.

'That sailor we met in the evening was rather different, wasn't he?' Dee asked me suddenly.

'I was waiting for you to mention him! Why do you say different?' I asked, now very interested.

'He didn't ask for our numbers, he wasn't a pile-on, he just enjoyed his coffee and went his way. Isn't that weird?' she said.

'He is different, a nice kind of different. You don't have to be mean to everyone you like just so that they back off, you know,' I said a bit warily.

'I wasn't mean to him.' She bristled defensively. 'I was like I am with everyone, nothing different.'

'You know what I mean—you could just lower that guard for a bit, admit that you like someone, flirt a little. Dee, you are in the middle of nowhere; who knows if we'll ever come back to this place! Talk to people, have fun, loosen up, let the place work its magic on you, give it a chance, you deserve it!' I said. She just stared at me for a long time, without saying anything.

'Dee, I just want you to have fun and be happy.' I broke the silence first. 'Just promise me you will, and I shall end this sermon.'

'I promise I will let loose, have fun and be your kind of happy, okay?' she said as she heaved a sigh and rolled her eyes. 'Anything to shut you up right now.' I hugged, said goodnight and crawled back into bed.

The next morning, just as we had decided the day before, we got up early and got dressed. I was taking Diana flying! I was super excited, but she didn't seem on the same page as I. 'How are you going to fly, you are hurt.'

'I am going to be a passenger just like you; I just want you to fly in the small four-seater training aircraft. It is not like flying in those biggies,' I explained.

'Are they safe?' she looked at me with rounded eyes.

'Dee, I have over two hundred and fifty hours of flying them, without a single incident, that's how safe they are,' I threw up my hands in exasperation.

'That's how safe you are, Em, not the aircraft.' Dee still wasn't comfortable, I could see that plainly. 'Okay, I'll just take you there: if you aren't comfortable, don't fly,' I placated her and she nodded in relief.

Elijah drove us to the flying school. I could see the aircraft parked at the aprons. It reminded me of the flying school where I had got my CPL. It had a very large fleet of very old training aircraft. I missed those training days the most. Ask any pilot in the world and they will say, 'Those were the best days of my life!'

We walked in to meet the owner. Captain Sergio had already been told about us. 'Good morning, Captain,' I wished him as I shook his hand, 'I am Captain Meera, I was told to see you about a sortie.'

'Good morning! Garcia called me last evening. How is fatso?' He was smiling.

'He is good.' I smiled back.

'I will take you up myself, since you will not be flying. We will head out on a 172, is that okay with you, Captain?' he asked.

'That would be just perfect, sir,' I replied and looked at Dee.

She still wasn't happy with the thought of flying on a tiny aircraft. I held her hand and led the way towards the parking bay. We climbed into the aircraft after the pre-flight was done; The Captain and I sat in front while Dee sat at the back. I gave her a headset and told her how to use the mike. Before we took off we were told that we could not fly the regular circuit pattern because there was a British Petroleum ship docked, and we were bound by rules not to fly over it. So we would just go southwards and get an aerial view of the place.

Dee had been unusually silent all the while that Captain

Sergio and I were discussing the weather and wind direction. That didn't bother me because I knew how this was going to end. We started rolling out and the moment we left the ground and took off, I heard her scream into the mike, 'Woohoooo!! This is crazy, but I am loving it!'

We were flying low at 3,000 feet, so that we could get a better view. Captain Sergio showed us our hotel, pointed out the mall and then we flew over the sea. I had done this before but it still gave me the same thrill; flying over the sea was something else. Besides, flying simply made me feel free. I was at home up there, in a cockpit.

At one point early on, I used to quote the Canadian Spitfire pilot John Gillespie Magee (1922–1941), who flew in World War II's famous and decisive Battle of Britain. 'I have slipped the surly bonds of Earth,' wrote Magee, 'and danced the skies on laughter-silvered wings; sunward I've climbed…' to which I would add, 'But I'm still not satisfied.' I may since have stopped agreeing with Magee about the earth's bonds being surly—and you have to grant it to him, he was flying during World War II when things couldn't have been any surlier—but the rest of it still fits me to a T. I wanted Dee to feel the same; and this was only possible in small planes. The freedom you got with them couldn't be paralleled by the big jets. 'Are you having fun?' I turned to ask her.

'This is the best thing I have done in a long time, Meera, this is simply super!' she replied excitedly. 'No wonder you are addicted to this.'

'It is a different high, one that can never be experienced on the ground,' I said.

'Everything looks so different from up here, so tiny and insignificant,' she whispered reverentially, 'like it doesn't matter how tall or big you are, from up here it just doesn't matter.'

'It's the way you look at things, babe, everything begins to appear tiny after a certain height and then it disappears after that. The view from the top changes the way things look!' I nodded.

'This does change everything,' she said. After that she was silent for the rest of the flight. We landed after an hour of flying. Captain Sergio insisted on buying us a drink. Since it was too early in the day to even think alcohol, we chose to have juice instead and raised our glasses in a toast.

'To defying gravity!' I said.

'To taking chances!' Dee finally spoke.

Serendipity

After that exhilarating experience I decided to take Dee out for lunch. Mexican cuisine was our favourite comfort food. I asked around and found that there was a Mexican diner called Uncle Sam's not very far from where we were. We reached the place in ten minutes. It wasn't as fancy as I had been told. 'Are you all right with eating here?' I asked Dee.

'Sure! Any place for a good burrito, babe!' she replied promptly, just as I had expected. We walked to the counter and placed the order and while I was paying for it, Dee said, 'What are the odds?' I looked at her enquiringly and she pointed in the direction he was sitting.

'The sailor from yesterday'!' I exclaimed. Dee was smiling and so was I. 'Do you want to go say hi?' I asked. 'Nope!' she said. That ended the discussion; so we just walked to an available table and sat there waiting for our order to be called out. I was fidgeting with my phone when the man behind the counter screamed, 'Two burritos, order on the table.' Dee walked up to the counter to get it for us, but the handsome sailor was there first. 'Hi Diana!' he said.

'Hi Captain, you remember my name!' she said. 'And I don't even know yours.'

'Where I come from, forgetting a pretty lady's name is a criminal offence.' He smiled winsomely. 'My name is Aryaman Rathore.'

'Thank you, you are very liberal with those compliments, I must say,' she said blushing as she picked up the tray with the burritos on it.

'I absolutely don't mind you taking those burritos, but just so you know, the meat in it is lamb,' he said, smiling.

'I am so sorry,' she said, her face flushed, 'is this your order? I didn't realize...how foolish of me to just pick it up without asking ...' He was still smiling when she put the tray back on the counter. 'You can stop smiling now, Captain, it was just an accident.' Dee's tone was a tad acerbic.

'It is no accident, Diana, it's serendipity,' he said, and when Dee just looked at him, he added kindly, 'A sign from above.' Dee looked ready to give him a blistering set-down. Perhaps he saw that too, because he quickly asked, as though to divert her, 'Do you believe in them?'

'Signs from where?' she asked in a very, very cool tone, 'And for what? No, I don't believe in them. I picked up your order by mistake and that's all there is to it.'

'You don't think that some things happen for a reason? A girl from a thousand miles away meets a sailor who could have been anywhere in all the seas of the world, twice in two days, both times by accident—what does that mean to you?' He was still smiling.

'It means that the sailor is a flirt and a good one at that, but this time his ship has run aground. It also means that I am going to take my order, walk back to my table and enjoy my lunch.' She picked up our order which had arrived by now and walked towards the table.

'It was very nice meeting you again, Diana,' he called out to her retreating back, 'don't believe me now, but soon you will!' He waved at me as she sank into her seat and I waved back.

'What was that about?' I asked her.

'He thinks our bumping into each other twice in two days was serendipity, no accident,' she told me drily.

'He has a point,' I said carefully, as I unwrapped my burrito.

'Whose side are you on, dummy?' She scowled.

'On the side of truth, as always,' I mumbled with a big bite in my mouth. 'Let's for an instant consider what he has said: it isn't normal, you said it yourself Dee, what are the odds ...' I finished.

'This is life, stupid, not some romantic movie. These things don't happen in real life,' she insisted. 'It's a coincidence, that's all.'

'Yes, coincidence is a possibility, but I like the sound of serendipity better,' I said.

'Finish your food, Em, and then let's go back and have a lie-in for the rest of the afternoon. I am already tired with the flying and all—don't know how you do it every day.'

'Fine, I won't take his side! And I shall buy you a drink in the evening at that interesting place in the bay area,' I said as we walked out and got into the car.

Elijah dropped us back to the hotel and within minutes of reaching the room, both of us were on our beds, tucked in for the afternoon. The love of afternoon siestas was a common one, just like a million other things. The plan for the evening was decided. We were going to a place called Pier One. It was the most famous place in the area.

→

When I woke up Dee was already dressed to kill in white. 'Heels or flats?' she asked me when she saw me get out of bed.

'Heels. Why didn't you wake me up?'

'You looked happy while you slept, I didn't want to interrupt your dream.' She chuckled.

I gave her a hug and then I asked, 'What should I wear? I can never decide.'

'That pink dress we got from Chanel, that colour looks very nice on you,' Dee said. I just took her at her word.

Pier One looked like a shack, though it was the biggest one I had ever seen. It was right on the beach, with a bar in the centre running all the way across the place. The barmen were wearing bright orange shirts and big smiles, flaunting their skill, swinging the bottles around. On one side was a large stage with a live band and a bunch of attractive girls dancing to 'Buttons' by the Pussycat Dolls. The crowd, mainly sailors, I guessed by their crew cuts, and some tourists, were enjoying the performance thoroughly.

On the other side was an array of pool tables surrounded by men holding beer mugs, cheering and making a ruckus. Just ahead and towards the sea were tables set with lovely flickering candles. From the options we had, our choice was clear. We walked towards the pool tables. 'We would like to book a table for ourselves,' Diana said to the man in charge.

'You will have to wait for forty minutes, madam, why don't you get a drink for yourselves at the bar till then?' he replied.

'*Kya karein?*' she said, asking me what we should do until then.

'Are you up for a little fun?' I asked.

'Obviously!' she said. 'What do you have in mind?'

'Let's play pool!' I said and walked towards the first table in the line. She looked at me and knew exactly what I was up to! I looked at the bunch of men playing at the table; they were decently dressed and sounded British. I glanced back at Dee for approval and when I got the nod from her I said to the one holding the stick, 'Would you mind terribly if we played with you guys?'

'Do you know how to play?' he asked, looking rather surprised.

'A little,' I said, 'how about a bet, losers buy beers?' A round of laughter rippled through the throng, by which time the balls had been arranged and the guy handed me the stick.

We had been at it only for ten minutes when we won our first round of free beers. The look on their faces was worth a whole lot more. We now had a crowd watching us, some cheering for us and others for them. Three games, all straight wins, later we made another deal with them. 'The winner keeps the table,' Dee said.

'You can have the table, ladies, we shall drink away to the storm that hit us, that was brilliant!' The man said in an accent I would kill to have.

'Why, thank you!' said Dee, adding in a conciliatory tone, 'do let us buy you a round of drinks at least!'

'That is very gracious of you, but we shall pass. Enjoy your evening!' The men wound their way through the crowd as they waved cheerily to us. I gave Dee a high five and started setting up for another game, this time just between us, like we used to play back home. I was walking around the table collecting the balls from the pockets when a voice startled me: 'Ladies, would you mind terribly if we played with you?'

'Hello, Captain,' I said, trying to appear composed though I was about to giggle. 'What a pleasant surprise!' I shook his hand and wondered what Dee would have to say about this third serendipitous meeting.

'It certainly is,' he said gravely. 'This is my friend, Captain John.'

I smiled at them and glanced at Dee who was walking back from the bar carrying our drinks. 'Hey, look who's here,' I said to her.

'Have you been following us, Captain Aryaman "Unusual" Rathore?' she said, trying very hard to hide her smile.

'No, ma'am.' He shook her hand and looked like butter wouldn't melt in his mouth. 'It's just an accident, if I may add: a very fortunate one at that.' And he winked at her! 'Are you pretty women up for another bet?' he said in the same breath.

'I am game,' I said in a hurry, not giving Dee time to refuse.

'What are we betting for?' I continued.

'One wish,' he said, 'it could be anything under the sun and over it, obviously the winners get to make it, okay?'

'Sounds all right,' Dee replied, much to my surprise, 'just that the wish can't be anything illegal or immoral; simple change, hope you're okay with that?'

'This is getting very interesting—can we make it a best of three? I kinda like it when the suspense builds up!' I said.

'Let's play already,' said Captain John.

'Irish,' I whispered in Dee's ears, 'forget the bet, honey, I just love his accent.' She gave me a glare and we began to play. The crowd around us was having its share of fun. They were hooting and cheering and also sighing at every shot we took. The first game ended with Dee and me winning.

'This wasn't bad at all, eh, Em!' She was teasing the Captain now. 'We won again!'

'Yes, we haven't lost a game since we got here, Dee! I love this place,' I replied. The men just smiled and sipped their beer while we were making a fuss over winning another game. The table was set again, the game started but this time Captains Rathore and John were playing much better than they had in the last game. They waited right up to the last ball to pocket their victory. The audience went ecstatic cheering the new winners. 'Lucky shot,' said Aryaman, 'but it makes the score even,' and he smiled wickedly.

'And now for the decider, ladies,' said the Irishman. Both of us smiled at them and at each other with supreme confidence. We were not just good winners but also graceful losers. Besides, we had another game to win it for ourselves. The table was set again. I got to make the break and potted a solid—balls numbered 1 to 7 are usually referred to that way—and then two after that. One missed chance from me and Aryaman came in. He potted four consecutive striped balls—those numbered 9 to 15— with all shots qualifying as extraordinary. Dee then took her stick and swayed around the table potting two more and missed.

The Irishman looked like he had done this a thousand times before; he walked across and potted the two he could easily. I knew I could finish the game for us; I just had to pot two solids and the 8 ball. I did just that, but I missed the 8 ball by a whisker. Dee sighed audibly. Aryaman walked by me, pinched my cheek and then went on and potted the one striped ball and the 8 ball in the next one minute. 'Well played, Captain!' I said.

'Indeed,' Dee was smiling, 'a very well-deserved win.'

'Thank you, ladies!' he said as John shook hands with us. 'Should we settle the bets over dinner then?'

'Yes please,' I said as we walked towards the beach. The four of us sat at one of the tables by the beach. We ordered dinner, after which Dee and Aryaman made small talk and John excused himself to go to the washroom. I took off my shoes and gestured to Dee that I was going for a walk. Walking barefoot on the beach was therapeutic for me, the soft sand under my feet took away all the exhaustion. The wind blowing in from the sea was playing carelessly with my hair. I just kept walking till I touched the water. It was surprisingly cold, and it sent a chill through me. I wrapped my arms around myself as I gazed at the sky, the moon staring back as it always did. On the far horizon moonbeams poured in silvery rays on to the water and rippled towards me before melting into the black velvety sea. I could have just stood there forever. I turned around when I heard Dee laugh. She seemed to be enjoying herself; Aryaman was making her laugh, I loved him for that. She looked at me and waved, asking me to come back. I walked back to the table, leaving a picture perfect world behind me.

Dinner was served and consumed over another session of pleasant conversation. I learnt that John was from Ireland and his family actually owned a castle back home. He also told me that all Irishmen could indeed sing very well! After dessert Aryaman finally said, 'So I guess it's time we got our wishes granted!' He was smiling. 'I'll let John ask first,' he concluded. We just nodded. 'I would like Captain Meera to take me up in her aircraft, but only if it is not too much of a hassle,' said John looking at me.

'It would be a pleasure, Captain John, but I am grounded because of an injury, although I could certainly take you up when I'm flying as co-pilot! It would be a lot of fun,' I answered honestly.

'I would love that,' he said.

'It is an unforgettable experience, you can take my word for it, Captain,' Dee said. 'And what is your wish, Aryaman?'

She turned towards him. 'I would like you to give me one day out of your life,' he said, looking intently at Diana, 'one full day with me; one chance to show you this place the way I see it.' Diana just nodded, looking spellbound.

'Should I pick you up tomorrow at 8 then?' he asked softly. She nodded again!

The Surprise

The phone rang exactly at 8 a.m. Diana smiled and picked it up. 'Good morning, my lady,' Aryaman said. 'Are you coming down, or should I come upstairs?'

'I'll be there in five minutes,' she replied, trying to hide her smile. She looked pretty in a yellow summer dress and leant over to hug me. I was snuggled in bed and did not want to get out of it. So I just extended my arms. 'I don't feel very nice leaving you alone, what are you going to do all day?'

'I am a big girl, Dee; you don't have to worry about me. I am going to catch up on my sleep, order in and laze around,' I answered indolently as I stretched in bed.

'Call me,' she said, kissing me on my cheek.

'I won't!' I said, winking at her conspiratorially.

She waved and pulled the door shut behind her. I drew the comforter over my face, closed my eyes and prayed that she would have a nice day, and dozed off again.

I was startled awake by the ring of the telephone. I checked my watch, it showed 10:30 a.m. I had slept for two and a half hours, but I could have easily slept some more. I dragged myself reluctantly out of bed and answered the phone.

'*Magandang umaga, Kapitan*, you have a visitor, he is waiting for you in the lobby,' said a very cheerful voice.

'Good morning, a visitor? But I am not expecting anybody,' I said to her while I tried to think hard who it could be. 'Okay, I am coming downstairs,' I said and hung up.

I hated early morning visitors since forever. They make me grumpy. I was still trying to think who it could be as I looked for my footwear under the bed when the phone rang again. In all the confusion I hit my head on the side of the bed. I was already fuming. 'Tell me,' I said peremptorily into the phone.

'Your visitor is waiting for you, madam,' the cheerful voice on the other side said again.

'I will be there in two minutes, and please don't call back. Let him wait!' I said grumpily. I walked out of my room, dragging one foot behind the other. I was still in my shorts and tee from the last night. A chirpy bell boy crossed me on the way to the reception. He smiled at me and said, 'Good morning.' I just smiled back; it was too early in the morning for me to make small talk.

The lady at the reception pointed to my visitor standing at the far end, by the gate. Great, the man had his back to me. The sun was so bright that I had to squint to see him—the rays were bouncing off his silhouette. He was wearing a black linen shirt and blue jeans. 'Excuse me,' I said and as he turned, my heart stopped beating for a second. I couldn't believe what I saw.

He walked towards me and I stood there dumbfounded. He looked as amazing as he always did. The stubble was new, making him look even better. He was dragging a tote bag behind him. He put his arms around me, picked me up and then kissed my cheek. All I could do was smile, it was unbelievable. He then put me down as gently as he had picked me up.

'Oh my God, is this even real!' I exclaimed. 'Aditya, what the hell are you doing in this city, no wait, what the hell are you doing in this country? Why didn't you tell me you were coming? How did you know where we were staying?' I continued, without pausing for breath.

'One question at a time, sweetheart.' He smiled. 'I am here to give you a surprise. I took a flight to Manila and then another one arranged by Captain Garcia to Subic. Ding picked me up at the airport and got me here.'

He put his hand on my waist, turned me around in the direction that I had come from and continued, 'I will answer all the questions you are going to shoot at me as I have a beer in an AC room. Okay?'

'Oh yes, so sorry, I am still a little lost,' I said.

'I usually have that effect on people,' he said with a straight face. I punched him on his arm as we walked towards mine and Dee's room. He held my hand and kept holding it. He was the same Aditya I had grown up with, in all his glory and warmth, but there was something different about him. I just could not put my finger on what it was. I sat on the bed cross-legged while he washed his face. 'The stubble looks good,' I said.

'I know!' he replied.

'Are you going to tell me what you are doing here?' I said, making a face at him.

'I will tell you the truth, but you won't believe me, Em!' He was now sitting on Dee's bed.

'Try me,' I said.

'I will sometime,' he said smiling.

'Nonsense!' I retorted. 'C'mon, Adi, tell me! When I asked you to come, you said you were busy and couldn't leave just like that and now you are here.'

'I told you, I will tell you but you won't believe me.' He was laughing now. I threw a pillow at him in exasperation. I didn't know why he was here and for how long, but it felt great to have him there! So I didn't push it much. He called for his beer while I got dressed.

'Now that you are here, what do you want to do? Should I tell you the options that we have?' I said.

'I have a few things on mind,' he said, 'but first, come here and show me your leg.'

I walked up to him and put my injured leg on the bed. He touched it softly and asked, 'How badly does it hurt, Captain?'

'It's much better than it was, doesn't hurt much. But I am not supposed to strain it anymore,' I replied and moved away hastily. His touch on my knee gave me goosebumps. 'Okay, so whatever we do, we have to keep that in mind, right? If it hurts even a tiny bit, just tell me.' He said as he looked at me just a second longer than usual. I nodded.

'Get dressed, we leave in ten. I have called Ding, he will be here any minute,' he said.

'Where are we going?' I asked.

'Someplace nice,' he said.

'I am asking so that I can dress right,' I continued.

'Wear whatever you are most comfortable in,' he said, finishing his beer in one long draught. I got into a pair of shorts and pulled a tee on top. He was talking on the phone to someone. I looked into the mirror to put on some kohl and noticed a smile on my face; it had been there since morning! Within the next ten minutes I was ready, waiting for Ding to bring the car around. Ding smiled at me and said, 'Good morning, Madam.'

'Good morning, Ding,' I replied, 'I am sorry you had to cut your vacation short.'

'This is my job, madam, I like it,' he said as he shut the door after I sat in the car. Aditya sat beside me; he had already told Ding where we were headed. 'Did you tell Mum you were coming over?' I asked.

'Only Rhea knows I am here to see you, everyone else knows I am here on business,' he replied.

'Hah! So you are here for work! What kind of business would you have in this part of the world, Mr Banker?' I asked, bursting with curiosity.

'We are financing a pearl farming project in the country, it needs my approval,' he said with a straight face.

'You are almost heading marketing and sales for the whole of South Asia,' I said excitedly, 'that is not bad at all.'

'I know,' he said and he kept looking outside the window. Aditya had always been very sure of what he wanted and also how he was going to get it.

We continued driving on the road hugging the coast. I kept talking to him about everything from the engine-failure incident to how Dee had gone on a date with Captain Aryaman. He listened intently but did not talk much, as usual—just a 'hmm' and 'okay' intermittently. This is how he had been since I had known him. I was now used to this and so was he!

The car pulled over in front of a resort. 'We are going scuba diving,' he said, 'it won't hurt your leg at all, it's not a very deep diving site, therefore no pressure on the body, and it also will give your leg a much-needed workout before your medicals.'

'You have really thought this through,' I said as we walked

to the reception. He did not answer. It was all still like a dream to me. I couldn't believe he was standing there talking to the man at the counter. He walked back with another man. 'This is our diving instructor, Jose,' he said to me, 'and this is Captain Meera, she has the injured leg I told you about,' he told the man.

'No problem that is,' said Jose in all the English he knew, 'just follow instructions.' I smiled at him. He walked us to the boat we were to take. There was another man in it too. Aditya got on first and helped me on to it. As the boat zoomed off it was clear that the captain of our boat knew just where to take us. I sat looking at the brilliant shades of blue spread out all the way across to the horizon. 'I love this,' I said to Aditya. 'It's something I always wanted to do!'

'I remember you telling me that.' He smiled. I smiled back. 'There is something different about him,' I thought, 'or perhaps it's just me!' I dropped the thought. Jose walked towards us and said, 'The diving suits are on the lower deck, you have to change. We will be there soon.'

We took a flight of stairs to the lower deck and found the diving suits piled on top of each other. I changed into one, in one of the changing rooms. Aditya was already back up by the time I was done. Jose began to instruct us on what we were going to do. Since the sea wasn't very deep, it was a very basic training we had to take. He told how to use the oxygen mask and that it was almost like swimming. The boat had stopped moving now.

'This is the entrance to Subic Bay,' Jose said. 'Ahead of us is the sea and behind us is the bay, we will dive here. This place is very popular.'

'What are we looking for?' I asked.

'There are many treasures here, everyone sees a different one. You tell me what you saw when we come back.' He winked at Aditya. I made a mental note of asking Adi what that was about once we were back.

'You have a monitor on the device in your hand, we are going down to 43 metres,' Jose said, pointing at the black band on his wrist. 'We jump on the count of three. Glasses in front of eyes—check!' We nodded. 'Turn oxygen knob to on—check!' We nodded again. 'All set!' And we nodded yet again. 'Three, two, one,' he counted and gave us the signal to jump. I was a little nervous and I looked at Aditya; he gave me a pat on the back and then a thumbs-up. That's all I needed. He then held my hand and we jumped into the sea. The oxygen tanks we were carrying on our shoulders were heavy enough to plunge us down instantly.

It took me about a minute to get used to the feeling, but when I did, the scene around me left me stunned. It was a shade of blue that cannot be seen from the surface. Sunlight looked different inside water. There were fish in colours that I had never seen before. Some of them got a little too close for comfort. We kept going deeper into the water. I kept checking the monitor for the depth we were at. Aditya stayed just an arm's distance from me; he had done this before and was not as uncomfortable as I was. He kept signalling to show me the beauty around us. I was too busy exploring the place for myself. We were about 30 metres into the sea when he touched my shoulder and pointed at something below us. The water was a little murky, which meant we were almost at the seabed. I could not make out what I was looking at, but it looked like something big.

'A capsized boat perhaps,' I thought. I swam in that direction hurriedly. And all of a sudden, out of nowhere it appeared! I was so excited to see it that I let out a scream! It was an aeroplane!

An aeroplane at the bottom of the sea... It seemed like it had been there for a long time. The current at the seabed kept swaying us gently while we checked out the wreck. It was a McDonell Douglas F-4 Phantom II, a tandem-seat combat aircraft used in the 1960s. The paint was completely off, so it was hard to determine which country it belonged to. It just sat there silently, in all its pride, alien to the environment.

I moved towards it, touching every part of the fallen angel. The wings were still sturdy, but the body was frail. There were weeds growing in and around, fishes swimming where the pilots once sat, all of these denizens of the sea trying to make it a part of their world. The sight was breathtaking, and vivid.

I knew in that moment that this was a sight I would never forget. I had absorbed every bit of what I saw. I looked around and saw Aditya. He was looking at me as if he understood what I was thinking. He held my hand and led me back upwards. The sight slowly dissolved back into the ocean as we got on to the boat.

'Did you find a treasure?' Jose asked, smiling at the look on my face.

'It was so beautiful that saying anything about it might ruin it,' I said.

'You don't have to say anything, your eyes are saying it all,' Aditya said.

'Thank you so much for this, I will never forget it,' I said as I hugged him impulsively. He held me tight. I could feel the warmth of his arms wrapped around me. His face was on my neck and I could feel his breath on the side. It sent a chill down my neck. I moved away awkwardly.

'You should change before you fall sick and ruin my trip,' he said and I snapped out of something indescribably exciting and yet strangely unknown. 'Yes,' I said and walked to the lower deck.

We had always shared a comfortable physical proximity but it had never felt awkward till today. Aditya had always been very liberal with hugs, but the ones that I was getting today were different. There was a funny feeling in my stomach. 'Must be the diving,' I thought aloud while trying to unzip the zipper of the wet suit.

After struggling with it for over five minutes I knew I wasn't going to win. The zipper was stuck, and I needed help.

I called out to Aditya. He was still in his diving suit. I told him I needed help. He fidgeted with the runner for a second and then pulled it lower. I was scratching my shoulder continuously. He took a step towards me and without saying a word, lowered the zipper to my chest, and then moved the side a little off my shoulder. He moved his finger over my collar bone and said something. His voice got lost in my heartbeat. I had never before heard it beat like that. 'Don't worry, it's just a rash,' he said, looking at me. I couldn't think of anything to say, so I smiled.

I changed into dry clothes and gave my heart a minute to settle before I went back up. We got back to the shore. Ding was waiting for us. I checked my phone which I had left with him. There was a missed call from Dee. I called her back.

'Why didn't you answer your phone?' she demanded.

'You won't believe it if I told you,' I said cheekily.

'Where are you?'

'Forget about me, I am fine! Tell me about your date!' Diverted, she said, 'I can't believe I am saying this, but I am actually having fun! We plan to see you for dinner, so don't vanish on me again.'

'We'll talk at dinner, and don't call me again, go have fun!' I said.

'I will!' she said and hung up. I got into the car beside Aditya, and Ding started the car. 'I hope you didn't tell her I was here,' Aditya said.

'No, I want her to be as surprised as I was!' I replied with a grin, as we pulled over close to a tiny, shabby-looking shack. 'What are we doing now?' I asked, looking at the shack. 'Lunch,' he smiled.

I was very hungry, but more than a little sceptical about the place we entered. It was small with tin tables and plastic table covers. There were a few locals drinking. The Pinoys had no designated time for alcohol; they could drink anytime, every time and all the time. Aditya pulled up a chair that screeched as he drew it to the table. I sat opposite him. 'Are you sure you want to eat here?' I asked, 'I can take you to a better place, you know.'

'Yes, woman, I am sure,' he answered.

'But why?' I made a face.

'By the end of the meal, you will know why!' He signalled to the server and ordered an array of seafood. All I could hope was they also served chicken, because that was the only meat I was comfortable eating, with mutton a close second. Seafood and I just never got around to being nice to each other. 'What chicken preparations do you serve?' I asked at the first chance I got.

'Yes, yes, chicken ng dagat.' The server was smiling.

'Please get me one of those with white rice, okay?' I asked.

'Yes.' He nodded profusely.

When the food was served we had a lobster and a crab on the table amongst some fish submerged in curry. I was still waiting for familiar-looking food to be served. What was served to me looked like the oriental cousin of butter chicken. I was used to the flavour by now and so I went ahead and dug into the rice. It tasted very different and very yummy. I was halfway through my meal when I decided to offer some to the man who was very elegantly making his way through a huge lobster.

'You want some?' I offered.

'Nope, I am good,' he said.

We continued eating. The dive had made me hungry, so I overate and ended up feeling quite bloated. But I was happy with the food. The place was way too underpriced, I thought, as we paid the bill and moved to the car. 'That was a nice lunch, thanks,' I said to Aditya.

'Yes! But I didn't think I could get you to eat seafood without making a fuss over it,' he replied with a grin.

'I did not have seafood, Adi, I had chicken,' I said indignantly.

'Yes you did, you had chicken ng dagat, which means chicken of the sea, my friend—tuna!' He was laughing now.

'Whaaat!' I was surprised. 'How do you know this? And why didn't you tell me that when I was ordering?'

'I know it, because it was written on the board of specials with ingredients. And of course you didn't bother to read it!' He was still laughing. 'And I didn't tell you because I wanted you to get over the stupid mental block you have against seafood—it's healthy and good to taste!' I just shook my head in disbelief.

'How did the tuna taste?' He was teasing me now.

'It wasn't bad,' I answered, 'the only thing that is bad is you, Aditya, you are the meanest meat I know.'

'I agree,' he said, 'but stitched together with good intentions!' he added.

I smiled and looked out of the window, feeling quite lazy now and craving a snooze. I saw we were headed back to the hotel; so there was a chance I could sneak a short nap. I was in love with the day. I had already had three lovely surprises and it wasn't even evening yet.

The Lighthouse

I was woken up by someone talking in a low voice. It was Aditya, standing by the window, watching the setting sun as he talked into the phone. He saw me wake up, and ended the conversation politely. 'Did I wake you up?' he asked, while walking towards me.

'Not really,' I said.

'Chai?' he asked as he pinched my cheek gently.

'Yes please!' I said. He called room service while I got up and washed my face. 'You are being awfully nice to me, Adi,' I said in jest, 'what's going on?'

'I am always nice to you, Em, it's just that you are suddenly beginning to take notice,' he replied. Maybe that was true, but I didn't know what to say to that and so I changed the topic. 'I think I should call Dee before she makes some elaborate plans for the evening involving me!' I said.

'I think you should let her plan. We will surprise her wherever she is,' he replied. I nodded and called her number. 'Hey Dee! Am I disturbing you?' I said.

'No, stupid,' she said amiably.

'Okay! Before Aryaman hates me more, tell me: what is the plan for the evening?' I asked.

'He wouldn't hate you, he just told me a little while ago, he really likes you,' she said in a teasing tone.

'Tell him I like him too, but I think my best friend likes him more.' I laughed.

'Shut up and listen, you mad woman,' she retorted, 'meet us at the lighthouse at 7.30; it's a famous place, and the driver should know how to get you there.'

'Are you sure you want me to come?' I said, pulling her leg, 'because if you don't want me to, you just have to tell me, you know!'

'Meera, you're mad. Just be there,' she said and hung up. I told Aditya the plan for the evening; he listened, his eyes glued to the phone, multitasking as always. 'Did you hear what I said?' I asked.

'As always, I did,' he replied. 'If I am not looking at you, it doesn't mean I can't hear you.'

'Yeah, yeah, whatever,' I grumbled.

'Now get dressed, Captain! Let's go and surprise your best friend.' He winked at me cheerily.

The lighthouse was at the end of Subic city on a cliff overlooking the sea. It had been there for over a hundred years. Civilization had slowly crept up around it, and now there was actually even a restaurant at the base. It was one of the places I was looking forward to seeing.

I opened my suitcase, looking for something to wear and automatically picked out a black dress. Sometimes I thought the colour of my blood was black—the colour had ruled my wardrobe forever. I was dressed in thirty minutes. All I needed was my black stilettos and kohl in my eyes! Aditya was wearing a white shirt and a black jacket over blue jeans. 'You look pretty, Meera, you should dress up more often,' he said.

'Thank you, have you called Ding?' I said, sidestepping the compliment.

'He is waiting for us,' he answered, shaking his head as if he understood just what I'd done.

The drive to the place was surreal. The road curved and turned its way into the forest on the mountain. There was no light except that from the car. The moon played its part perfectly. An ethereal ivory hue seeped through the trees. The forest followed us till we could see the end of the mountain. The lighthouse stood at a distance, drenched in white, a silent spectator to the romance of nature around it.

We stopped at the entrance. The place was dimly lit. I couldn't wait to see Diana's reaction to the surprise. I was taken aback when Aditya opened the door of the car instead of Ding. He then placed his hand on my waist as we walked in. The breeze from the sea was warm, but I had goosebumps on my arms.

I saw her sitting, facing away from us, at a table in the corner. Aryaman sat across her, his eyes sparkling in the candlelight. He looked our way as we entered. I placed my fingers on my lips and signalled him not to tell. I walked up to them, with Aditya just a step behind me.

'Hello beautiful!' I said to her.

'Finally, Her Highness arriveth; we have been waiting for you! What took you so long?' she said.

'I took time finding a date for myself,' I was smiling.

'Hello Diana,' Aditya said.

She sprung from her chair and turned around. 'Aditya! How is this even possible?' she said excitedly. 'When did you get here? Meera, why didn't you tell me he was here, we could have met earlier,' she said, giving him a big hug.

'That's exactly why I didn't tell you,' I said. Aryaman was standing by, watching our little reunion with a smile on his face. 'Adi, let me introduce you to Captain Aryaman, he is Dee's date!' I said.

'I have heard the story,' Aditya said to him, shaking hands.

'After spending a day with the lady here, I have heard a few about you too,' he replied, and turned to me, 'You look nice, Captain'.'

'Thank you! Now if we are done with the pleasantries, I would like a drink, please!' I said.

'Wine for me,' said Diana.

The conversation at our table flowed smoothly, only interrupted now and then by gusts of laughter. There was a glow on Diana's face telling a tale that did not need words. When the men stepped out for a smoke, we got our chance of a quick round of catching-up. 'What is Aditya doing here?' Dee asked.

'He wouldn't tell,' I said, 'but I am sure he is here on work.'

'So he was working all day, while you slept?' Diana was curious.

'He hasn't touched his laptop since he arrived, we went scuba diving,' I said.

'That doesn't seem like work to me!' She was teasing me.

'Can we talk about you please, tell me everything!'

'My day was amazing, every single minute of it was beautiful. We went sailing on a yacht, deep into nowhere. It was just us and the seagulls and the open seas. I have this feeling that is alien to me, Em! I have never felt like this before. Funny, eh?'

'Trust me,' I said, 'I know exactly what you are talking about!'

'Aryaman and I are so different. He is a believer and I am a sceptic by nature. He is so carefree and lives life at will, and I go by the rules and do things a certain way. His life has no rules, no boundaries; mine is contained in a lot of ways. It's like we belong to two different worlds, and yet there seems to be a connection between us.' She went on, 'I am a free spirit scared of being bound by feelings, of even expressing them, and he doesn't think twice before talking about them. Being caged scares me, I'd rather fly. He isn't even scared of getting hurt. I told him he's like a happy fish swimming in an ocean of possibilities, but I am a bird who returns to the earth no matter how high it flies.'

The men returned. Aryaman looked at me and said, 'If you don't mind, I'd like to borrow your friend for a dance.'

He then held Diana's hands and led her to the dance floor. She looked like she was under a spell. 'Isn't it nice to see her like this?' I said to Aditya.

'It is,' he agreed, 'he seems like a nice guy. Do you want to dance?'

'No,' I said, 'I'd rather watch.'

They danced away, holding each other, the electricity between them palpable from where we were sitting. They were close, yes, maintaining a distance—Diana a perfect lady and Aryaman a perfect gentleman. The song over, they walked back to the table, still holding hands. Conversation over dinner swung from ships to aircraft and fashion to banks. We were all so different from each other; the only thing common at that table was the smile on our faces.

'This is all I needed to be happy! Great friends, amazing

conversation, good food and a chocolate truffle to top it,' I exclaimed.

'Who knew the four of us would be sitting here together.' Diana laughed.

'This is much better than what I had planned,' I said, 'I am glad we bumped into you, Aryaman.'

'The pleasure is all mine,' he said.

'But I guess it ends here,' Diana said. 'We are leaving tomorrow.' She was looking at Aryaman as she said this.

'Perhaps this isn't the end,' he said, 'it could just be a beginning!' He winked at her.

'Are you done with that?' Aditya asked me, pointing at my half-eaten dessert.

'Yes! Do you want some?' I asked.

'No! Come with me,' he said as he stood up, 'I have to show you something!' I got up, he took my hand and we walked towards the spiral staircase that went up into the lighthouse. 'Where are we going?' I asked. 'Someplace nice,' he replied. We kept climbing till we reached an opening in the wall. It took us to the deck. From where we were standing, we could see the whole bay on one side and the sea on the other three sides. The waves were hitting the rocks, making music and the moonlight danced on the water. Everything around us was in complete harmony. It was one of the most beautiful sights I had ever seen. 'This is perfect!' I said to Aditya.

'It is,' he said, staring far away into the sea.

'I still can't believe you are here though!' I said.

'I am here, Meera.' He turned towards me and ran the back of his hand down my cheek. His eyes held mine, 'I am here because I missed you, I am here because I would rather be here with you than anywhere else in the whole world,' he said. 'You have always been special to me, but I've realized you are part of me and I came here to tell you this.'

I could not think. I could only feel his warm hands holding my face. I moved into his arms and rested there. 'I'm glad you are here,' I said. He kissed my forehead and we walked down the stairs. Aryaman insisted he would drop Diana back, and so we drove back in different cars. Aditya and I did not speak a word on the way back. My head was clouded with thoughts and voices, the commotion a stark contrast to the silence outside. So many questions flashing across like neon lights: 'What's happening here? What does he really feel that he is saying all this to me?' What should I do now? Will I lose my best friend if I didn't share his feelings? I felt something different this time, but that needn't necessarily be the same as what he felt. What is this different feeling, is it love? Is Aditya in love with me? If it was love I would have known, so this isn't love, or is it? What's going to happen after this?'

I shut my eyes and put my head back, trying not to think and failing miserably. I really liked Aditya, but I wasn't in love with him. I knew I would have to tell him that. I was just hoping it would not ruin what we had grown up with. We reached the hotel, Aryaman and Diana right behind us. We would probably not be meeting Aryaman anytime soon so I got out to say goodbye. We shook hands and hugged each other. 'You will be missed, Captain,' I said.

'You shall be missed greatly too, Meera,' he replied, 'you are a delight to know.'

'Please keep in touch, with me as well.' I winked.

'I shall.' He smiled. Aditya said his goodbyes too, short and crisp. I glanced at Diana, and she nodded. We walked towards the room, leaving them on the porch. They kissed. She moved away. He handed her a box and then he got back into the car. She waited until his car was no longer seen. She then walked into the hotel, touching her fingers to her lips, holding the box with both hands. It was a blue velvet box; she opened it. It had a chain with a dolphin pendant on it. There was a note in it signed by Aryaman. It said: 'What'll happen if the bird were to fall in love with the fish?'

Woman on Top

Three very sleep-deprived souls were seated in the car by ten in the morning. Each of us had spent an indifferent night, and it showed on our faces. Diana looked tired, ecstatic and sad all at the same time. She had twisted and turned all night, next to me, on the bed, unable to get over the day she had spent with the man who had changed something in her. She had donned the chain the moment she got back to the room. She showed us the note that Aryaman had given her. Adi had smiled and said nothing, I just hugged her tight. Now she was sitting in the car, looking outside the window, playing with the pendant without even noticing it.

Aditya looked content and calm. He was the only one smiling. He had worked on his laptop through most of the night, keeping Dee and me up with a gentle flood of small talk. He hadn't mentioned anything about our conversation on the deck again, but the way he looked at me had changed subtly. He was sitting in the front with Ding, playing music on his iPod, and answering calls on his phone.

I was hiding behind my aviators, hoping the confusion on my face would pass as sleep deprivation. After getting back into the room last night, a surge of emotions had hit me all at once, but mostly I was guilty that I didn't feel the same way as Adi did. I was also scared that I might have to make a very difficult choice, which would cost me my best friend. I wished I could speak to Dee about it, but she was in a world of her own and I didn't want to reach out to her about this. I was upset because I hadn't told Adi how I felt yet and he had taken my silence in a different way. I was staring into my book without reading a word, finding it difficult to concentrate for once.

The voices in my head were thrown off kilter by my phone ringing. It was Captain G. 'Good morning, Captain Meera,' he said, 'how was the surprise I sent your way?'

'Good morning, sir!' I said. 'The surprise was great! We are on the way back now. Am I seeing you in the evening?' I asked.

'You, madam, are seeing the company doctor for your medicals at 17.00 hours. Call me as soon as you are done seeing him,' he replied.

'Wilco, sir, thanks,' I said and he hung up.

We entered Manila in the next four hours. Dee was out of her trance by then and was excitedly showing Adi some of the things she had already seen in the city! 'Wait till you see Captain Meera Khanna's apartment!' she said excitedly and he smiled.

'What are we doing in the evening?' he asked me.

'I have a medical appointment at five at the company office. You guys get some rest while I get that done,' I said.

Aditya nodded. We parked at the Pink Pearl and Ding went into his usual drill with the concierge. The liftman greeted us like he always did. I was back to being Captain from being just Em for all these days.

'Welcome to my humble abode,' I said as I opened the door to the apartment. 'All I can say is that I am proud of you,

Meera!' Aditya exclaimed. 'I told you, it's brilliant!' Dee joined in. 'They treat her like a royal, and she behaves like one too!' I smiled at their excitement, pushing away all that was in my head. I had the upcoming medical occupying my focus now. I just wanted to get back into the air, flap my wings, feel the air around me and leave the earth behind. That was my happy place, the place where nothing else mattered. I was a little concerned because getting back from an injury as fast as I was going, was a little difficult. It took months for some. Although my leg felt fine now; I was hoping it stayed like that.

'What are you guys going to do while I am gone?' I asked.

'I will make Sadu here watch a movie with me!' Dee replied.

'Good idea, how about watching *300* again!' Aditya was standing with his hand on my shoulder.

'I have it on my laptop; you can call a pizza for dinner. I think I will be back by then,' I said.

'We are so not watching *300*! I say, let's see *P.S. I Love You* again!' Dee said.

'Oh no, no, no, I can't handle all the crying that comes along,' Aditya said.

'We'll see who wins,' said Diana as she walked away. 'There is a box of tissues on the table,' I told Aditya, 'I already know who is winning this one!'

'And I always thought you were on my side, Em,' he said.

'C'mon, Adi, be nice to her. Dee is already missing Aryaman.' I winked at him.

'Both of you shut up, or prepare to be beaten up,' Diana said, holding up a pillow threateningly.

'Don't be shy, Dee, tell us you miss him,' Aditya teased as he walked towards the bed.

'This is war!' Dee said, and hit him with the pillow.

'This is Sparta!!' he replied and the fight began. Before I knew it I was a part of it, and just like that everything was back to the way it was supposed to be!

I was sitting in the company office waiting for the doctor to arrive, lost in thought and moving my leg unknowingly. He walked in just after five.

'Good evening, Doctor,' I said, sounding as confident as I could.

'Good evening, Captain! I am sorry you had to wait for me, but I have a feeling it's going to be worth it,' he said reassuringly.

'I hope so too,' I said.

'We shall do a stress test with you after I have checked your leg,' he said, 'if you can move it the way you were doing while I walked in, it should be fairly easy, I think.' He was smiling and now so was I.

He checked my leg and seemed happy with it. The stress test had two parts, I was supposed to run on a treadmill at an incline for forty-five minutes and then do a flight on the simulator with the doctor as my passenger. Halfway through the run I was a little exhausted, but I was glad my leg wasn't hurting at all. The doctor kept monitoring my performance. His face gave away nothing while he was doing his job—a perfect poker face. After running for the required time, he asked me to stop and re-examined my leg. He then wrote something down in his notepad.

'Where are we flying to, Captain?' he asked me.

'I shall take you on the same flight as the one in which the incident happened, Doc,' I replied, still breathing heavily from the run.

The company had one of the best Flight Training Devices (FTD) installed. It felt nice sitting in a cockpit again, even if it was just a simulated one. It hadn't been more than fifteen days since I had flown last. I was in my element and therefore nothing could go wrong now, I thought. I started the engine on sim and we took off—that did not take any effort. Every part of my body knew what it had to do and it was doing exactly that. My leg was working on the rudders making minor directional changes effortlessly. Twenty minutes into the flight, after I had tamed the machine to act like I wanted it to, I glanced at the doctor. He seemed to be enjoying his ride!

'This is all good, now show me something you would never do in an aeroplane.' He smiled.

'You are one awesome doctor!' I said. 'Fasten your seat belt, we are going to have some fun.' By the time we were done, I had shown him everything that could be done with a plane but should never be done officially! We had done barrel rolls, loops and spins, wheel washed in the sea, flown below the Golden Gate in San Francisco and over the Alcatraz, even landed in front of the pyramids in Egypt. We flew over India and I showed him the Taj Mahal. When the ride was over, he got off and handed me a sheet of paper. It was my medical report. It said 'Fit to fly' in red! Captain Garcia was the first person I called.

'I have the medical report in my hand, sir,' I said to him.

'Just tell me what the remark section says.' He seemed anxious.

'It says I am fit to fly!' I said, almost screaming in excitement.

'Congratulations, kiddo! I am very happy!' he said.

'So am I! Finally I shall be up in the air again! Gravity sure sucks,' I replied.

'Call scheduling first thing after you hang up, so that they can put you on a flight ASAP,' he said.

'I will do that, sir,' I said.

'I am so glad you are back! You have some willpower, I must say! This calls for a party, let me make a few calls and fix it all up,' he said and hung up. I called scheduling and told them about the report, and then I called Aditya. 'How is the movie coming along?' I asked.

'Gerard Butler is dead, his wife is moaning, Dee is crying and I am eating pizza,' he said. 'How was your medical, when do you get the reports?'

'Well, I am fit to fly. So I guess the medical went well,' I said.

'Oh, that is great news; fly back and we shall celebrate,' he said.

'I am on my way,' I told him.

Since the tension about the medical was over, my brain was back to finding a way for the other important thing I was supposed to do. I was thinking of the best way to tell Aditya that I cherished his friendship so much that I didn't want anything to ruin it, not even love. Also, that I had worked very hard to reach where I was. I had a fixed flight plan as far as my career was concerned and I wasn't ready for any diversions yet.

By the time I reached home I had come to the conclusion that there was no right way to put it. I was going to tell him what I had thought without mincing words. What he decided after that was totally his call. Just like I was the pilot-in-command of my life, he had the controls of his.

Dee was already holding a glass of Baileys when I walked into the house. She gave me a tight hug and handed it to me. Aditya hugged me too and then kissed my forehead.

'Today we drink to Captain Meera's return to the skies,' Dee said dramatically.

'Here's to you, sweetheart! And here's to your undying spirit. May the fire in it always burn and light your eyes up like this forever,' Aditya said dramatically.

'Thanks, both of you! Let the binging begin,' I grinned and raised my glass.

After a whole night of celebratory drinking, and mixing all kinds of alcohol available, we all woke up with the mandatory hangover. It was the last day that Dee and Aditya were spending in Manila, their flight back home was booked for the day after. We were determined to make the most of it, and so Dee and I decided to blackmail Aditya into making breakfast for us. He was too hungover to fight back, and so he agreed without putting up much of a fight.

He made us a coffee that he specialized in; he called it the 'morning after shot'. It was extremely strong and sweet at the same time. It had the potential to kill the effect of the shots one had ingested the night before! One full mug of coffee and a few French toasts later, we were back to a nearly human state. The plan for the day was made. We were going shopping at the Mall of Asia and then later catching a movie if time and enthusiasm prevailed.

Getting dressed took away almost all the energy the breakfast had garnered; I was already dragging my feet. Coffee would have to be administered intravenously through the day if I was to survive without becoming a casualty. 'I need some more coffee,' I said grumpily. 'So do I,' said Dee, gripping her head with her hands.

'Stop cribbing, ladies! Let's go get you some coffee, although it's not going to cure your hangover,' Aditya said.

'I know it won't, but it sure will help me keep my eyes open,' Dee retorted, 'now walk!'

'Em, don't forget your shades and that Saridon,' Aditya reminded me. I just smiled at him as I shut the door.

We were shopping for stuff that Diana wanted to take back to India. Walking around with my café mocha from Starbucks, I was still a little dazed. My phone buzzed. I read the message that Captain G had sent. 'Throwing a party for my favourite First Officer who has not only bounced back from an incident without a scar and is now fighting fit, but has also logged 1100 hours of flying. Please be there at my house at 19:00 hours with your friends.'

'Captain G has invited us to his house in the evening,' I said to both of them. 'What's the occasion?' asked Aditya.

'He is throwing a party for me, I think people from the company are invited,' I said.

'Another party?' Dee said, 'Damn! Now I have to buy something to wear to it!'

'Oh great, another reason to shop,' sighed Aditya.

'We don't need a reason to shop, but I don't mind if there is one.' I smirked.

'Don't worry, Sadu, we shall get you something too!' Dee said, as she pinched his cheek.

'I don't need anything!' he snapped.

'It's not about the need, Adi, it's about the want,' I said, mimicking Dee. 'What am I wearing?' I asked her.

'Something not black,' she replied and walked towards a store.

'Women!' he said, and walked behind us, shaking his head in mock-dismay.

We reached Captain G's house at seven. Ding was also invited to the party, so he walked right behind us as we entered. Everyone who I knew was there, along with everyone who knew me. The party apparently had begun a while ago; people were already getting refills for their drinks. We walked up to where our host was standing.

'There you are,' he said, spotting me.

'Yes, sir,' I said smiling. 'This is very nice, thank you.'

'You are very welcome, kiddo,' he said to me and then he turned towards Aditya.

'You must be Prince Charming.' They shook hands. 'And you must be Lady Diana,' he said to Dee.

'He is Aditya, the man who conspired with you to surprise me,' I said.

'I liked what he was doing, so I helped him do it.' He patted Adi's shoulder. 'Let's get the ladies and you something to drink,' he continued. The men walked away. Jenny walked towards us looking like a doll, dressed in a black miniskirt. She had met the men at the bar and so she was carrying our drinks. I introduced Dee to her, they hit it off at once. Fashion did to connecting women what cigarettes did to men. I took that chance to walk away and meet a few people who were smiling at me.

I met the loaders and the dispatchers standing together and then walked towards the maintenance guys. I got to know that Nefertiti was almost back up and that we would be able to get her back in the air in a day or two.

The night cruised on; people started getting drunk and the conversations louder. Captain G wasn't letting go of Aditya, but Aditya seemed to be enjoying the conversation. He occasionally looked in our direction, as if to see if we were okay. We were being entertained by Jenny, who was telling us the story of how she met the Commander. For the first time in forever, Dee was interested in someone's love story. She was curious and I was amused!

Amidst all the commotion, I suddenly heard Captain Garcia's voice; he was clinking his glass and calling for everyone's attention. The room gradually fell silent and he spoke: 'I would like to raise a toast to Captain Meera Khanna. She not only handled the plane very efficiently during a critical engine failure, but she also kept her cool when it was most needed. She was grounded due to the injury the landing caused on her leg; yet she has managed to make a quick comeback and as you can see, she is not limping anymore.' A round of laughter went across the room. 'So Meera, here's to you,' he turned towards me as he spoke, 'I know it's not easy to stay far away from home on an island country with quirky people like us, but there is a benefit to it too. You are at 21.00 hours, which is the first checkpoint in your life, but you are the highest-qualified woman pilot in our country. You are the woman on top!'

People were clapping and I was overwhelmed. Dee hugged me in glee and so did Aditya. I walked up to Captain G, thanked him and then hugged him. Ding opened a bottle of champagne and poured it for all of us. Aditya raised his glass and repeated the words that I knew would always make me smile, 'Cheers to the woman on top!'

As the cheers died down and people got back to their drinks and conversations, almost all eyes were off me, and I was breathing normally again. The feeling was now sinking in. I wasn't where I wanted to be, yet, but I knew I was moving in the right direction. Something else, however, still needed resolving, and I knew what I had to do. I gulped down my drink in a hurry and told Dee I was going out to get some air. She was happily talking to Jenny and Captain G, so she didn't mind. I asked Aditya to follow me. We walked out of the sea-facing bungalow, crossed the road towards the sea, found a bench next to the walkway and sat on it.

'That was quite a speech Captain G gave,' Aditya commented.

'Yes, he dramatizes things a little,' I replied.

'I like him,' he said, 'and I am so proud of you, Em.' I just nodded. Neither of us spoke for a minute. Then I took a deep breath and began: 'I have to tell you something, Adi—I am so glad you came over. The timing was just right, you got to see my world and be a part of it. I always wanted to make you proud of me, and it felt really nice when you said that.' I was looking at him. 'Aditya, you are the best thing that has happened to me after flying, but I am not ready for anything more than what we already have. It has taken a lot of effort and patience to be where I am in my career right now, and I would want to stick to it until I make commander. Giving you false hopes would kill me; so…I had to say this.'

He kept looking out at the sea, his expression unchanged. I was still looking at him, trying to read his thoughts—in vain. The one minute of silence that passed between us was so loud that it deafened me. 'I think we should go back,' he finally said. We walked back to the house in silence.

Just before we entered the house he said, 'You know the best thing about friendship, Em? It doesn't have break-ups.' I hugged him tight. My best friend was back.

Mother India

'This is the last and final call for passengers on Qatar Airways flight to Mumbai,' said the woman on the PA.

'Call me when you've landed,' I told Dee as I kissed her cheek.

'I will; you take care of yourself, I love you!' She hugged me back.

'Stop turning this into a Bollywood scene, you are in touch twenty hours of the day on BBM, video chat and whatever else, so just get on with it,' Aditya interrupted impatiently.

'I am going to miss you,' I said to him.

'I'll miss you too, Meera,' he said. I saw something in his eyes that I didn't understand, but even before I could work it out, it disappeared. 'Listen to me, Em,' he said in a serious voice, 'be safe! I will shoot you, if you get yourself killed, understand?' He was smiling. They walked into the terminal, while I walked towards the car. I had never felt this alone before. The emptiness was making its presence felt, now more than ever. Prolonged exposure to this state would be harmful to my state of mind, so I knew I had to get over it as fast as I could, and I knew exactly what would make it all better. I dug out the phone from my pocket and dialled the number.

'Yaad aa gayi maa ki, remembering your mother at last, eh?' the voice on the other side said.

'I think of you always, Mom.' One sentence from her and I was already feeling a little better.

'Has Diana left?' she asked.

'Yes, I just dropped her off at the airport, Aditya is also flying back.'

'Must have been fun with them, and now you are back to being alone,' she went on, 'just a little bit of alone time, beta, you will be happy the moment you sit in the cockpit!'

'I know, Ma,' I said.

'What have you sent for me?' She changed the topic.

'Nothing!' I giggled.

'Okay! Will Diana deliver the "nothing" or will Adi come?' She was laughing, and so was I.

'Dee will call you,' I said, still giggling. 'Now I have to go, Ma, will call you soon!'

'All right,' she said.

'I love you, Mother India,' I said.

'Don't call me that,' I could almost see her wrinkling her nose. 'It makes me feel old. I love you too!' she said and I hung up.

My mother had been my strength and succour since the day I was born. Her voice had a calming effect on me. What we spoke was usually just a camouflage, while our souls connected deeper and had their own silent conversation. I didn't have to tell her what I felt, somehow she always knew. She didn't have to tell me that she was there for me, every cell in my body felt it. She had not just created me, but had also made me what I was.

✈

After Dee and Adi left, it took a while but life came back to being normal. The normal that I was used to, the normal that had existed before the engine had stalled. I was fit to fly and finally so was Nefertiti. The weather had cleared up completely. The typhoons had left no traces in the air, but the land still bore the ravages of devastation. I was amazed by the audacity of us humans. It had not even been a month since the storm and the travellers, intrepid or otherwise, were back. Backpackers, tourists in groups, even honeymooners. Most of them very interested in visiting the places we had evacuated people out of. I was told by Captain G that there was a new term coined for what we were seeing, it was called Post-disaster Tourism. I didn't care what it was; as long as I was getting to fly, I was a happy kid!

My routine was gradually going from slow to fast, and from there to hectic and finally to crazy-busy. I liked crazy-busy. I would come home almost dead, eat and sleep. Dee was back to being the busy bird that she was. Aditya was back into his world. We spoke once a day at least and video chatted whenever we could.

Mom called every time I landed, and updated me with everything that she thought I should know of, from how the stupid neighbour was mistreating his dog, to Chandrayan, India's first unmanned lunar probe, discovering water on the moon! Everything was back to where it was. I was loving it! My aim was set and I was inching towards it with every take-off. The flights were regular and more comfortable than what we had seen in the recent past. I was getting better at landings and Captain G's stories were getting more interesting.

We landed after one of our usual flights to Cebu and back. As always, Captain G left the shut-down to me as he strolled out for his regular shot of nicotine. I got the job done and walked out, a little after him. We spoke about the flight, got into the crew cars and left the tarmac, like we did every time; but there was something that was unusual about today. My phone hadn't buzzed. I tried calling my mother, and it went unanswered. I said my goodbyes to Captain G as Ding carried my bag, still dialling my mother's number.

My mother not answering her phone was Code Red Level One for me. She had done it in the past; she had sometimes forgotten to carry her cell phone when she went out buying groceries, but I freaked out every single time with the same intensity. My cool subconscious mind was trying to tell my hyperventilating conscious mind that it was not an emergency till it actually was one, but the latter was too busy making up theories to listen.

As a war raged in my head, I was still dialling her number, now very impatiently.

'Where are you, Mom?' I muttered urgently after dialling for the twentieth time, hoping she would hear it. Still no one answered. I had been trying for the last forty-five minutes. I was positively worried now and my anxiety was beginning to border on fear.

She could have forgotten her cell at home, or she must be sleeping or she could be in the washroom, I thought. She had replied to my 'taking off' text with a 'good luck' about five hours ago. By the time I was dropped home, it was taking me all my might to stop from screaming out loud. I was now one stop short of sheer panic. With every passing minute I was losing it.

Now at home, I was sitting on the bed, still in uniform, too preoccupied to even take my shoes off as I dialled Aditya's number. Adding to my dilemma he did not answer the call too. I waited for the 'will call you back' message from him, that didn't come either. There were panic alarms jangling at full volume in my head. There were a hundred ways this could have been justified, but somehow it didn't feel right. I knew there was something wrong. I kept staring at the phone, not being able to think straight in my panic-ridden state of mind. I decided that I should call Dee.

'Hey Em, how was the flight?' she asked.

'Hey Dee, flight was okay. Mom isn't answering her phone, I have called over twenty times, there is something wrong I am sure,' I said, all in one breath.

'Oh, don't worry, babe, I am sure she is fine.' She tried to calm me down.

'Adi isn't answering his cell either, doesn't usually happen like this, you know,' I gasped.

'Breathe, Meera, he must be in a meeting or busy somewhere. I shall call his office and find out. You calm down,' she said.

'Call me the moment you know anything,' I said and hung up.

I knew I had to calm down. So I dragged myself off the bed to change. While I was washing my face my phone buzzed. I ran out of the washroom, bumping my shin on the table towards the bed where I had left my phone. It was a text from Dee: 'Aditya left office in a hurry, said there was someplace he had to be. I am trying Aunty's number. Will call you soon.'

None of it was making sense. I called Mom again and it went unanswered. I was so far away that there was nothing I could do except wait and hope everything was okay. A thousand questions crossed my mind all at once. Where could

Mom be? Was she supposed to go somewhere? Was she unwell when she last spoke to me? Why wasn't Aditya answering? Where was he?

I was still fidgeting with the phone in my hand, looking at random pictures and going through my contact list. I saw Rhea's name on the list and dialled immediately. Rhea was the cuteness-and-innocence dose to my life. She was a happy little ray of sunshine. Looking at her reminded me of myself! We had similar eyes that sparkled with mischief, a smile that gave off warmth on a cold day and never-depleting optimism. Talking to her gave me hope. She was also Aditya's kid sister.

She answered the phone in her chirpy voice, 'Hello MD, it's been so long since we spoke. How have you been?' she said. MD was short for Meera Didi. 'Heya kiddo, I have been thinking of calling you forever now, but something always comes up,' I replied, trying to sound as calm as possible.

'That's all right! Are you okay, you sound different?' she said.

'Do you know where Adi is?' I asked. 'Mom isn't answering her phone, so I thought I would ask him, but he isn't answering either.'

'I haven't spoken to Bhai since last night, he usually calls after he gets back home from work,' she said, sounding a little tense now.

'Maybe it's nothing, but if he calls you, ask him to call me ASAP, okay?' I said.

'Don't worry, it's all going to be good and you will be laughing over all this soon,' she said.

'I hope so too, you take care, I shall talk to you soon,' I said and disconnected. It had been over eight hours of torture and my head was splitting. I was lying on the bed with my eyes tightly shut and the phone on my stomach. I started and looked around after about a minute, the sun had set. I realized I must have drifted off to sleep. My phone had fallen on my side. I fumbled around for it and saw the red light blink. My heart went from 80 to 200 beats in that one instant.

It was a missed call from Aditya. I couldn't believe I had missed the call I had been waiting for. It was exhaustion. I called him back. 'Hey babe,' he said and I knew there was something wrong the moment I heard his voice.

'What is it, Adi? There is something wrong, I am sure. Just tell me Mom is okay,' I said.

'Aunty is absolutely fine, I am here with her, you have to relax. Everything is okay, Meera,' he reassured me.

'Why are you with Mom then, and not at work? Tell me Aditya whatever it is,' I insisted.

'It's Laika, she met with an accident in the morning, we got her to the doctor, they operated on her but she didn't make it through,' he said with a deep sigh.

I just sat down on the ground, as if my legs couldn't hold me anymore. My heart let out a tiny whimper. I was still holding the phone, as tightly as I could with one hand and wiping my tears with the other. Laika was the four-year-old Labrador who stayed with my mother. We had got her on Mom's birthday when she was about a month old; she had become the centre of Mom's world within the first day. I had named her Laika after the first dog that went into the orbit of the earth.

'How is Ma doing?' I spoke into the phone.

'She is very sad, I think you should talk to her now,' he said, and handed the phone to her.

'Hello,' she said and a chill ran down my spine.

'Hey Ma,' I said. 'I am so sorry about Laiku, I am so, so sorry.'

'I am sorry about her too, beta, she fought very hard, though she lost,' she said.

'I am sure,' I said.

'It happened so suddenly, I had no idea what to do, so I called Aditya. He came rushing and took care of everything. We just got back after burying her. It has been a terrible day. I am so thankful Aditya is here,' she said.

'So am I, Mom. Thank God for Aditya. You should get something to eat and rest. I shall talk to you in the morning.' I said.

'All right,' she said and handed the phone back to Aditya.

'Thank you for everything, Adi,' I said, 'thank you for being there, and taking care of Mom.'

'Stop talking, Em, get some rest,' he said. I did not have the energy to contest it. 'Thank you, Aditya,' I said again, 'for all that you have done. I know how difficult it is for you to leave office on a weekday, I am just glad you were there with Mom.'

'You are sleep-talking now, woman. Besides, I always had my priorities set. People who matter come before anything else,' he said gruffly.

'Goodnight, Adi,' I said in a tired whisper.

'Sleep well, Em, and don't worry about Mother India, she is happier with me than she is with you,' he said cheekily.

I laughed after a whole day of not even smiling. Two things I was sure of, Aditya Kapoor was a gem and he was going to be whacked by Mom for calling her Mother India!

The Bird and the Fish

I woke up with a start. My phone was ringing. It was too bright and way too early in the morning for my comfort.

I took the call without opening my eyes. 'Good morning, Em,' said Dee in her usual effervescent voice.

'What exactly is good about the morning, Dee? It's too early and I don't even have a flight,' I mumbled.

'I know, I know it's too early for you, but this is an emergency,' she said hurriedly.

'Emergency!!' I sat up straight in one instant. After the Laika incident I was a little jumpy.

'What's wrong, Dee?' I said 'Tell me. Quick!'

'Aryaman is in town,' she said, 'and he wants to meet me.'

'Oh dear God, Diana, you are one crazy woman. You scared the living daylights out of me! Which part of what you just said is an emergency?' I was fuming.

'Babe, you don't get it—we have been talking on the phone and video-chatting every day since we met in Subic,' she said.

'Hmm,' I replied with raised eyebrows that she couldn't see, thankfully.

'I have told him so many things that I haven't told anyone. We talk almost in all the spare time we have. We are continuously in touch with each other,' she continued.

'Hmm.'

'Are you awake and listening to what I am saying, Meera?' She was angry now.

'I am listening to you, Dee: you like Aryaman and he likes you too, he is now in town and he wants to meet you. You are scared of meeting because…okay that part I missed, tell me again, why are you scared?' I said in a monotone.

'I am not scared, I am never scared, and why should I be scared?' she mumbled back.

'Okay, so you are not scared, then why is it an emergency?' I asked.

'I don't know why it is one, but it just is one. Now help me get through this,' she said, with the or-you-are-not-my-friend hanging in the air.

'Dee, listen to me, take a deep breath and look at yourself in the mirror. You are perfect. The man likes you, for God's sake. There is nothing wrong with that. All you have to do is let him. Don't push him away, please. I know you like him too. It's a beautiful thing,' I said.

'It's all so new to me, Meera, what if this is not the right thing, what if it doesn't end up being perfect?' she said softly.

'It doesn't have to be perfect,' I replied, 'and you won't know till you give it a chance.'

'I am taking your word for it,' she said.

'Yes, please do, now tell me: what is the plan for the day, where are you going, what are you wearing?'

'He said he'd pick me up from home in an hour, and we'll take it forward from there.'

'Great! All I am going to say is have fun,' I said, 'and also, give me all the details when you get back home!'

'I will try,' she said, 'now you go back to sleep. I love you, Captain Meera Khanna.'

'I love you too, Princess Diana the Second,' I replied as I hung up with a smile plastered on my face.

Sometime later that hour Aryaman knocked on the door of the fifteenth-floor penthouse in one of the uptown localities of Mumbai. The maid answered it, asked him to sit and walked back into the kitchen. Aryaman looked around the pristine, centrally air-conditioned apartment. The maid walked back in with a glass of water, and with her came out one of the inmates of the place. 'What's his name?' he asked the maid.

'Santh Coopid,' she said in a heavy Marathi accent and walked away. Aryaman extended his hand in the direction of the huge dog; walked toward it and their friendship began. 'I am assuming your name is Saint Cupid,' he said to the Saint Bernard as he played with its long hair and the gentle canine loved every bit of it, 'I am Aryaman.'

Diana walked out of her room at this point, feeling very nervous but hiding it well. She was about to meet him after three months of getting to know each other virtually. She saw Aryaman sitting on the couch playing with her dog comfortably. Her heart skipped a beat just looking at him. He stood up when he saw her. 'I see the two of you have met,' she said, trying to sound as normal as she could. 'We have. He is a sweetheart and you are gorgeous,' Aryaman said as he walked up to her. Her heart was beating like never before.

Standing inches away from her and smiling he asked, 'Do I get that hug or what?'

'Hmm...what?' was all she could manage. He put his arms around her, she stood there awkwardly for a second, not knowing what to do. It took her a few breaths before she felt comfortable, and the moment she did, he broke away. She managed a smile. 'I have waited so long for this,' he said. His voice was warm, just like his presence in her house. 'Please sit,' she said, and walked towards the couch. He followed her and to her surprise, sat right next to her. Saint Cupid cuddled around his leg.

'He likes you,' she said.

'Don't you?' he asked. She felt her cheeks go warm. He saw her blush scarlet. 'What would you like to drink?' she asked, trying to get things back to normal. 'A good coffee sounds nice,' he said, 'does the maid know how to make one?'

'She doesn't, but I do,' Diana replied and she was back in the game. 'Would you mind if I joined you in the kitchen?' he asked. 'You are welcome to join me; coffee doesn't have a secret recipe,' she said. The three of them walked towards the kitchen. She stopped at the entrance, patted the dog's head, and showed him the direction he was supposed to go in. 'You are not supposed to be in here, baby,' she said. He trotted off obediently.

'One helluva obedient guy that is.' Aryaman whistled in surprise. 'He takes after his name, he is a saint and he spreads love all around,' she replied. She started on the coffee, and he stood there watching her move flawlessly. 'Did you do the interiors of the house by yourself?' he asked.

'Yes,' she replied in surprise, 'how did you know?'

'The house screams it out. It's beautiful and white,' he replied.

'White?' she asked curiously.

'Yes, white!' he said. 'You could use some colour around here,' he continued. She frowned, pouring the coffee into the mugs, handing him one. He took a sip out of his mug, and let out of groan of contentment. 'That is the best coffee I have had in a long time.'

'Thank you,' she replied, smiling.

'There are a hundred ways of getting coffee wrong and only one way of getting it right,' he said. 'I have a good feeling about this, Diana,' he said, sipping his coffee again. She burnt her tongue with a big sip of the hot coffee; she had heard him say her name for the first time. It felt like no one said it like this before. Like the name had belonged. She looked at him, he was watching her.

'A perfect woman who makes the perfect coffee, what are the odds?' he said with a big grin on his face. As they walked back to the couch, she looked at the man who was walking ahead of her. He was handsome and stylish at the same time, but he had raw edges to him, which he seemed to enjoy. It confused her. They sat there sipping coffee and catching up, right from where they had left off last.

He told her that he was on the shore for only a day, for official work in the country and that he would be flying back on a chopper to the ship, which was anchored a few thousand miles off the Indian Ocean. She told him about her work and how hectic it was getting. She explained the dynamics of her work to him.

While she sat cross-legged on her couch, listening to him tell his stories, she felt unnaturally comfortable, like she had never felt before. She was never fond of guests, but he didn't seem like one, even though it was the first time he was there. The intimacy of the experience was something that made her stomach tingle, like nothing else in the world did to her. Suddenly he stopped talking; the silence got her back from her thoughts. He edged closer to her and touched her neck. She shivered and moved away.

'That looks beautiful on you,' he said, pointing at the pendant she was wearing.

'It is beautiful, I have done nothing to it,' she replied, almost whispering.

'I haven't been able to forget the day we spent together in Subic, so I thanked my lucky stars when this work rolled out and I had to fly into Mumbai,' he said.

'It's nice to see you here, live.' She smiled back.

'Believe me, the pleasure is all mine,' he said, moving closer to her. The silence between them was shattered into a million pieces with a shrill voice from the kitchen. 'What do you want me to make for lunch?' it hollered.

Aryaman moved back on the couch, and Diana shifted uncomfortably as she replied, 'I'll just tell you, wait a minute.' She turned towards Aryaman—he didn't look the slightest bit put out by the sudden change of scenario while she on the other hand was heartbroken, though she had no idea why. 'What would you like to have for lunch?' 'There are some nice places nearby, we could have Thai, Italian, Mexican or even Chinese,' she continued.

'Can we have pav bhaji?'

'Pav bhaji!!' she exclaimed. 'I don't know of any places that serve that around here.'

'We could go out and look for it,' he said.

'Or we could ask the maid to make it, 'cause I wouldn't look very good on a newspaper with pav bhaji all over my face,' she replied.

'The editor of *Femme Fatale* spotted eating greasy food at a roadside stall!' He laughed. 'Sounds like a good caption to me.'

Diana walked to the kitchen and spoke to the maid for a minute before coming out, relief writ large on her face.'''' On the way back to where Aryaman and Saint Cupid were watching something very intently on TV, Dee picked up her phone and wrote '*He likes pav bhaji*' and texted it to Meera as fast and as discreetly as she could. Within the next minute her phone buzzed with a reply: '*I like pav bhaji too.*' Aryaman switched off the TV as she walked back into the scene.

'You could keep watching that if you want,' she said to him.

'I won't miss watching that when I am back on the ship, but I will surely miss talking to you like this,' he said. Her heart melted. Aryaman was back to being his chatty self in a moment. She liked to hear him talk. He told her about his family, that he was of royal lineage, related by birth to the king of Rajasthan. He spoke very fondly about his mom and also said that she was very sad when he had decided on leaving the country for a job. Diana was curious about the fact that he chose to spend the day with her instead of seeing his family, so she asked him. To which he very charmingly replied that he didn't want to interrupt his parents' vacation in Mauritius and also because he had something better to do.

Lunch was served on the dining table. It was a huge eight-seater glass table, with white legs. 'White,' Diana noticed and smiled. While the maid served the bhaji she noticed Aryaman asking for onions and lemon.

'Onions and lemon in the middle of the day!' She wrinkled her nose.

'What's pav bhaji without them, you should try some too,' he replied.

'I am good,' she said, using a spoon to eat.

'Try eating with your hands once, it will taste even better, trust me,' he said, and continued eating. The maid got back with chopped onions. He gestured with his hands to tell her the food was yummy. She blushed. Diana felt something flutter within. She watched him enjoy this simple meal of mashed veggies like it was the best on earth. A prince from la-la land was eating with his hands and loving it. What are the odds, she thought and laughed!

'Do I amuse you?' he asked.

'You confuse me,' she replied.

'Simple pleasures are what I miss on the ship,' Aryaman said, 'I can ask the chef to make the most exotic dishes and he does, but this is what I wouldn't get anywhere but here.'

She led him to the porch after they were done with the meal. He stood there looking out at the city stretching its arms below them. 'You have a beautiful home,' he said, looking at her.

'Yes, but it could surely use some colour,' she said, blushing.

'Don't you get lonely?' he asked.

'I don't have time for lonely! I have my work to keep me company,' Diana replied.

'When I am not working, I am on video chat with Meera or you,' she continued.

'Oh yes, video chat! The makers of that deserve much more than just money.' He laughed.

'What would you like to do in the evening?' she asked him.

'I have two tickets for a play at NCPA, would you like to be my date?' he queried.

'What's the name of the play?' she asked.

'Moonshine and Skytoffee,' he replied.

'I have no idea what that is.' She looked confused.

'You don't have to have an idea,' he said winking. 'It starts at 5 p.m., so I think we should be leaving soon.'

'Give me a couple of minutes to change and we shall be on our way,' she said and walked towards her room. Aryaman was standing by the window, lost in thought when she came back, dressed in a pink dress and matching shoes. 'Are you lost, sailor?' she said, catching him by surprise.

'No, ma'am! I am not,' he said, 'I am exactly where I am supposed to be,' and kissed her cheek. She smiled and walked towards the door. She stopped on the way to pick up the keys to her car, while Aryaman held Saint Cupid's face in his hands and said goodbye.

'What car do you drive?' he asked on the way down in the elevator.

'A Honda Accord,' she replied.

'Great! I have never driven one before, this should be fun,' he said.

'I am driving us there, not you, Captain,' Diana said firmly.

'No you are not, I am,' Aryaman replied.

'It's safer if I drive, I know the place better, we won't get lost on the way,' she insisted.

'It's more fun if I drive and who cares if we get lost, in fact I love the idea of getting lost with you,' he replied.

They reached the car; she opened the driver's side and slipped into the seat. He sat next to her, smiling at how his appeal and argument were not only rejected but also ignored. They drove through the crazy Mumbai traffic and reached the place a little before the play was scheduled to begin. The place was bubbling with people. She even saw a few familiar famous faces. They walked to their seats in silence.

Sitting next to him with their shoulders touching each other, Diana looked back upon her day. It had been 'unusual' if she had to sum it up in one word. She looked at Aryaman, who sat there like a knight in all his glory. She really liked him. He made her feel different. She fetched her phone out from her purse and texted Meera: 'He makes me feel funny in the stomach.'

'That is a very good thing,' came the prompt reply. She looked at it and smiled. The play began. She was very curious to know what the name meant. Aryaman told her that it was an amalgam of two stories by the acclaimed Malayalam writer Vaikom Muhammad Basheer. She soon realized that one of it was a love story between Kesavan Nayar, a Hindu, and his landlord's daughter Saramma, a Christian, and the other one was an unlikely love story between Sainaba, the daughter of a cardsharper, and a lovable rogue, Mandan Muthappa, who was a pickpocket.

She found it amusing how these two couples came together even when the odds were against them. It was a true believers' story, and for a sceptic like her too, it made perfect sense. Or maybe she had crossed the lines and moved over to the other side. She believed what she saw was beautiful; whether it was possible or not was another question.

The performances were noteworthy and the applause at the end proved how much they were appreciated. Aryaman led her out before the rush had started making the way to the doors. 'Did you like it?' he asked her as they walked towards the car. 'It was unusual, but nice,' she replied.

'Quite like us, don't you think?' he said.

'Yes, very much like us,' she said, this time looking straight into his eyes.

'Walk with me,' he said and she followed. They were now standing at the end of Marine Drive, looking at the sea and the sun setting into it. 'This is the most beautiful place in Mumbai,' he said, taking her hand in his. 'Would you like to sit here?' he asked.

'Ummm, sure!' she said, pushing her inhibitions aside. She held on tightly to his hand as she climbed the wall and sat facing the sea. He moved in beside her. He was still holding her hands in his. 'The sea and the sun are the two things that are most important to every sailor,' he said. 'The sea gives us everything we need and the sun gives us direction.'

'I remember you telling me this in Subic.' Diana smiled.

'Do you remember me asking you a question then?' he asked.

'What if a bird falls in love with a fish?' she replied with a questioning glance.

'Yes, that one,' he said, his gaze fixed on something far away.

'I don't know what happens then, Aryaman; I am a very practical person and in my world, the fish and bird can't coexist,' she replied. 'So if they fell in love, they would only hurt themselves and each other.'

He was smiling. 'If a bird fell in love with a fish, sweetheart, they would meet at the horizon,' he said, pointing to the golden line where the sea met the sky. Diana felt a chill go through her body. 'You are such a believer,' she said.

'I am! I believe in love and it's magic. You just have to believe and when you do, things you could have never imagined happen to you. They happened to me. I met this girl a few months back and now I can't imagine my life without her in it. I am sitting beside her, holding her hands, looking at the sun kissing her cheeks and thinking how perfect my life is right now.'

'Aryaman, we just met a few hours ago,' she replied, using all her energy to say that. She could hear her heart beating even in the commotion the waves were creating, her brain was on its own trip, and she thought she was about to faint.

'We have been spending every minute of our free time talking to each other; we have practically been living together, doll. I don't know if this is the right time, but I know there won't be a more perfect time to do this: so, will you marry me, Diana?' he said as he took the ring out of a tiny box and held it in front of her.

Diana's face flushed. 'You cannot be serious,' she said.

'But I am,' he replied, 'I even got a ring.'

'Oh Aryaman, you can't be doing this to me.' She gasped for breath.

'I am only going to do this to you and to no one else ever.' He grinned.

'I like you, I really, really, like you, I might even love you, maybe I do, but marriage... this is crazy,' she said in one breath.

'I know it's going to be crazy, with your family and mine and all the drama,' he said, shaking his head. 'Oh wait, did you just say you love me?' He grinned, his eyes focused on her. 'How's that for crazy!!'

Diana looked away for a second. His gaze froze her brain; she wanted to gather her thoughts before she said something. 'I am still in shock, I have no idea what to say to you,' she said finally.

'Then don't say anything right now.' He put the ring back into the box and handed it over to her. 'Keep this with you, till the time you decide. If you decide to marry me, wear it. If you don't, I will take it back, I promise,' he said. She took the box he was holding and kept toying with it for a bit. She needed to breathe. Her heart was swelling; her face was blank, not able to pick between shock and happiness.

'Look at me, Diana.' His voice broke into her chain of thoughts. 'Do I look like one of those creepy people who slash their wrists if their proposal is turned down?' he asked.

She just shook her head.

'Then don't think so much, let it all go, you will know what you want when the moment is right,' he said, holding her hand. She nodded in agreement, hoping to God he was right. 'Let me take you to dinner,' he said, changing the topic.

'Please, let me take you to a place I like,' she said. He agreed. She put the box in her purse and they walked back to the car. 'Do you know where the Taj is?' she asked him when she handed him the keys.

'I do,' he said.

'There is a small place called Bay View next to it, on the rooftop. They serve all kinds of food, and play good music; are you okay with that?' she asked.

'I could surely use a drink,' he said.

They drove in complete silence, Aryaman concentrating hard on not getting lost and Diana very aware of the rock in her purse. They were given a table almost immediately after reaching. This place was hidden in between two big hotels. It was an unusual combination of classy and quaint. They sat at the table overlooking the Gateway of India, while the music around them got louder and better at the same time. There were people dancing. Couples high on life and alcohol were making merry.

'Would you like to dance?' Aryaman asked Diana. She took his hand and they danced away to the music. With people cheering and joining in, it was quite a sight. He made her feel like a princess befitting the prince that he was. She loved the way he looked at her, the way he touched her. She was beginning to believe that there was something more than just 'like' there. The day had been a roller coaster, but she had lived every minute of it in happiness. She knew she was in love.

She moved closer to his ear and said, 'What happens if this bird falls in love with this fish?' She pointed at herself and then at him. 'They live happily ever after,' he said, swaying her as he moved.

'How?' she asked.

'They find a way,' he said reassuringly. It gave Diana hope, lots of it, but she still didn't know what to do about it. The song got over and they got back to their table. 'How are you so sure this is the right thing to do?' she asked him.

'I am not, I just know what I feel for you and with you, and I have never felt this before,' he replied.

'But our lives are so different; we barely are in the same part of the world at the same time. I can't leave the country, you can't leave the seas, how is it going to work, Aryaman? It is going to be so difficult,' she said.

'I am not saying it's going to be easy, I am saying it's going to be worth it,' he replied with a smile.

They clinked glasses to that. While they were sipping their drinks an attractive woman walked up to their table.

'You are a very good dancer,' she said. Diana looked at her to respond, but realized she was talking to Aryaman.

'Would you dance with me, please?' she said, batting her eyelashes at him.

'If my lady here doesn't mind, I don't,' he replied.

'Please go ahead,' Diana said in the calmest voice she had. They walked towards the centre of the hall. Diana felt like someone had put a huge load on her lungs, and they couldn't get air. She watched him move like the brilliant dancer that he was. She needed to talk to Meera, but decided on texting. *'I think I love him, I know I do. He has proposed marriage, I haven't replied, he is dancing with someone else, I can't breathe.'* Her phone buzzed in an instant. She dragged her eyes away from Aryaman only to see what Meera had replied. *'Woohooo! Dee, it doesn't get better than this. Take that leap of faith. You deserve to be happy! Go reclaim your man, speak now or hold you peace forever.'* Diana smiled; she knew exactly what she was going to do. She pulled out the ring from the box and put it on her finger. Then she walked up to the lady dancing with her man, tapped her shoulder, smiled and said, 'May I have my fiancé back please?'

The Maid of Honour

I was jumping on the bed when I got Dee's text about Aryaman proposing. My best friend was engaged—hopefully—and was going to get married. I couldn't wait to hear the whole story. I wanted to call her right away and ask, but I decided against it. Instead I dialled Aditya's number.

'Hey Meera, how are you?' he said.

'I am good; why haven't you been on video chat lately? Been a week since last we spoke properly.' I spoke in a rush.

'I have been a little caught up with things around here,' he said.

'I am sure you have been, I have so many things to tell you. Today's been a crazy day in India,' I went on.

'Meera, I am with someone, I will call you back the moment I can,' he said.

'Oh, I am sorry, I didn't realize I was interrupting, please go on. And call me when you can,' I said and I hung up. I was euphoric. There were two things that were stopping me from calling Dee and getting all the details right away. First was that she was still with Aryaman, and the second that I had an early morning departure. I pulled the blinds, shut the lights—

all this while jumping in glee—landed on the bed and forced myself to sleep. I had never waited for the morning this badly in all my life.

I woke up with a smile on my face and before the alarm. I showered, got into my uniform and called Ding: 'Good morning, Ding,' I said.

'Good morning, madam, I am reaching in two minutes,' he couldn't hide his surprise.

I waited for him in the lobby; he walked in a few minutes later, smiled at me, dragged my bag and led the way. 'Is it your birthday, madam?' he asked.

'No, Ding, Diana is getting married,' I replied, almost giggling.

'Many congratulations to her and to you,' he said as he drove me to the airport. I entered the aircraft after my pre-flight check. One of the loaders came in with the papers I had to sign. I looked at them and smiled at him. He was taken aback by my reaction. 'Mistake, Captain?' he asked.

'No, it's all good,' I answered and he walked away. Captain G entered soon after, making a face at me as he kept his bag to the side. 'Were you with someone last night?' he asked.

'No sir, I was alone! Why are you asking such an absurd question?' I asked back.

'There is "that look" on your face,' he said.

'Diana was with someone last night, and he asked her to marry him,' I said excitedly.

'That is good news, right?' he asked.

'Of course it is, sir!' I replied.

'Congratulations then! Now let's get this baby where she belongs.' We took off for Cebu. And after an uneventful landing into and take off from there, we headed back well in time for lunch. The first thing I did when we landed back was to jump out of the cockpit. Captain G was a little surprised, but he let it pass. I dialled Dee's number and jigged my leg impatiently while it rang.

'Hello Em,' she said groggily.

'Hello hello, rise and shine, my friend, it's a lovely morning,' I said.

'You are awfully chirpy, how much coffee have you had?' she moaned.

'Just the one in the flight, but leave me be, and tell me everything from the beginning,' I said.

'Can I wake up first and brush my teeth?' she said.

'No,' I answered.

'Okay, Em, what do you want to know, ask away!' She gave up.

'Is he still there?' I said.

'No, he left in the morning,' she replied.

'Yessss!' I was jumping. 'I mean, sad that he left, but good that he stayed the night,' I explained.

'Yess, I miss him already,' she said.

'I love what he has done to my best friend! Now tell me what happened.' I couldn't wait. She told me everything that had happened in the day, till the part where she sent me a text and I had replied and then she stopped talking. 'I replied to your text, and then?' I asked.

'Then I went and reclaimed my man by saying "Can I have my fiancé back?" to the woman who was dancing with him,' she said.

'That, my friend, is awesome...phir, phir?' I said. I was now sitting in the back of the car and Ding was taking me home.

'The look on both their faces was priceless. Aryaman held me in his arms and screamed "She said yes!",' she told me, the excitement of it all still ringing in her matter-of-fact narration. 'And then?' I pushed for more.

'And then we kissed, finished dinner and came home,' she replied.

'Oooooh,' I teased, 'and then?'

'Gah, Meera, and then we went off to sleep. Then he had a flight in the morning, so he left,' she said.

'Ohho, don't cut the story short, what happened after you reached home?' I asked.

'Meera, you are mad! I can't believe you are going to be my maid of honour,' she said.

'That I can believe, Dee, what I cannot believe is that you are getting married!' I was almost screaming.

I reached my apartment, changed and then the exhaustion from all the euphoria hit me. I pulled the blinds and made the room as dark as it could get. I looked at my call list. Aditya still hadn't called. I dropped him a text saying that I had just come back from a flight, and was off to sleep. He hadn't replied for the half minute that I was awake, before sleep caught up with me.

The next few days flew by me like happy white clouds. Happiness is contagious. Dee was happy and busy dealing with the new status. I was happy flying and making plans for her wedding. Aditya was busy with something and not available for either of us to chat with. The daily conversations between Dee and me had become different from what they used to be, we were now talking love—something that she was not ready for. We were also talking marriage, which I wasn't ready for. We were joined by Aryaman on one of those conversations; he wanted to talk to me about something very important, I was told. Seeing Dee and him together made me go 'awww' every single time. 'You guys look so good together,' I said.

'I keep saying it, but Diana doesn't believe me,' said Aryaman.

'Quit it, both of you, we have a situation here and you guys can't stop being funny,' Dee retorted.

'Okay, seriously now, what's the issue we are all gathered here to resolve?' I winked.

Diana opened a diary, turned a few pages hurriedly and said, 'So here it is: since Aryaman has managed to get himself a sixty-day leave, we need to speed things up. The dates that are available are the second of next month, that is fifteen days from now...how is that for you, Em?'

'Whaaat! Seriously!! That soon? I don't mind, if you guys don't mind,' I said, quite bowled over by the pace of the events.

'The sooner the better.' Aryaman winked.

'When do you want me there?' I asked Diana.

'Since you are the maid of honour and my best friend, you are needed here as soon as tomorrow. Will you be able to make it so soon?'

'Yes,' I replied, crossing my fingers.

'Great, it's all settled then, I shall take your leave now. Lots of love to both of you, and a kiss to you, Captain,' Aryaman teased.

'A kiss back,' I said and he logged out.

'Both of you are mad,' Dee said, 'and I love both of you so much.'

'I love you too, I am so happy for you, Dee. Now let me go and call Captain G and ask him for leave,' I said.

'Say hi to him for me,' she said.

Captain Garcia too was taken aback by the speed of things; just a few days ago I had told him that Dee had gotten engaged and now I was asking him for leave so that I could attend her wedding. 'When do you want to leave?' he asked me.

'At the earliest, sir,' I replied.

'I am okay with whenever you go, just come back as soon as the celebrations are over,' he replied.

'Thank you, sir!' I said. 'I promise I won't stay there a day more than I need to,' and I hugged him impulsively.

'Take care, kiddo,' he said in the warmest voice I had ever heard from him. I was booked on the next flight to India in the morning. I packed my bags with a smile on my face. I had called Mom and told her I was coming home; I had also left a message for Aditya with my itinerary details, since his phone was busy. Dee was more relieved than excited to hear that I was going to be with her through the madness.

I landed in Mumbai after catching up on the sleep that I had lost in all the excitement. I had received no confirmation about who was coming to pick me up. While the loader picked my bags from the conveyer belt, I checked my phone. There was no message from anyone. 'Very unusual,' I thought. I sent 'landed' to a preset group on the contacts. My mother topped the list here too. I had already decided on not calling anyone, taking a cab and heading home.

As I walked out, the salty, moist wind hit my face...I was back home, to the city that I loved the most in the whole world. There were people holding up placards with names, looking at the exit in anticipation. I walked past them and towards the taxi stand. I knew no other place better than this airport. It was then that I saw them: two men, looking as hot as it gets and a gorgeous lady between them. I was so happy to see them that a tear escaped the corner of my eye.

Diana hugged me and kissed my cheeks, her hug was the second best in the world; I was going to get the best hug next. Aditya stood there with a smile on his face, which could light up the darkest night. I hugged him tight. He just stood there letting me be in his arms for a whole minute. I moved out, smiled and walked towards Aryaman. As I stretched my hand across to shake hands with him he ignored it, hugged me tight and then he winked. 'Welcome to Mumbai, Captain.'

'This feels like heaven,' I replied, 'I almost thought no one was coming to pick me up!'

'Surprises are our thing, remember,' Aditya said. His voice was like music to my ears; maybe it was the lack of it in my recent past that was making it so special.

Dee held on to my hand as we walked to the car. As we settled in, I noticed that Aryaman was driving. I nudged Dee and signalled towards him. 'I am trusting him with my life, Em, the car is too small a thing to worry about,' she said. A huge round of meaningless giggles and lots of teasing ensued until we reached Dee's apartment.

It was already decided that I was going to stay with her and get things done around the city, till we had to leave for the wedding in Jaipur. My mother was to join us in Jaipur. It was all planned perfectly by Dee—she had convinced Mom how important it was for me to be around her and since Mom loved Diana as much or maybe more than she loved me, she had agreed to everything Dee said.

'*Aali ka Meera tu, kitti diwas zhaale tula baghun* (It has been so long since I last saw you, Meera).' The maid at Dee's house went all emotional in Marathi, and stroked my head lovingly.

'I missed you too, Maushi,' I responded in Marathi, adding,' I want pav bhaji too.' Maushi, as I addressed her, said affectionately, '*Tula je khaycha ahey sang, mi sagla banavnaar, tuzhya satthi* (Just tell me whatever you want to eat, I shall make it all, for you).' She couldn't stop smiling.

'Can we please take this inside?' Dee gently signalled Maushi to move from the entrance, which she had pretty much blocked. Meanwhile, Aryaman and Aditya were discussing the share market, totally oblivious to what was happening around them. I loved the camaraderie they already shared. They had so much to talk about, just like Dee and I did.

They kept at it through the day as we shopped for Dee's wedding dress and bought her trousseau. All we got out of them was an approving nod or a smile if and when there was eye contact. Aryaman was even staying at Aditya's house since he wasn't allowed to stay with Dee till they got married. The four of us were together from breakfast to dinner, after which the boys didn't mind dropping us back home and taking off for the night. We had all that was needed for a wedding in the three days that I spent in Mumbai.

The Fairy Tale

On the flight to Jaipur, Dee was visibly nervous. 'It's all going to be great.' I tried to calm her down.

'I'll be meeting his family for the first time, Em, that too a day before the marriage ceremonies start, who knows how it is going to be... Do you think we are going too fast?' she asked anxiously.

'Are you mad?! There is no need to be nervous at all, they are going to love you, everyone loves you. Look at that guy, he can barely keep his eyes off you.' I pointed in Aryaman's direction who looked at us across the aisle and smiled.

We landed in a city draped in sandy brown with red stonework all around. The pink in the Pink City was not really obvious, at least not at first sight. Aryaman, who had up until now let me do my 'best-friend duties' by being with Dee, now took charge holding her hand and walking by her side. Aditya and I followed as we exited the airport, with the loaders and our baggage in tow. There was a huge crowd outside, in the thick of it was a man wearing white clothes and a red turban who called out, 'Banna!'

Aryaman looked towards him and smiled. We were led a little away from the reception area by him, and that's where

I realized the grandeur of it all for the first time. Three black BMWs stood lined up one behind the other; the turbaned man instructed the loader to load the luggage in one. Aryaman then introduced us to him. 'This is Bhanvar Singhji, he manages things for my parents.'

'*Bhanvarji, yeh hain Diana, aapki baisa,*' he said, holding Dee's hand in his. He had introduced Dee to his manager as 'baisa'; 'bai', he explained, meant 'lady' and 'sa' was a honorific indicating notional and/or literal seniority in the hierarchy. In Dee's case it would be both.

'*Aur yeh hain Aditya, mera dost* (this is my friend, Aditya).' Aryaman patted Aditya's shoulder. '*Yeh hain Kaptaan Meera, baisa ki saheli* (this is Captain Meera, Baisa's friend),' he said, smiling at me.

Bhanvar Singhji folded his palms and bent down to his waist as he greeted each one of us. He then opened the door of the car that was second in line. Aryaman instructed Dee and me to sit in it. He and Aditya were in the leading car. I let out a deep breath as the convoy started to move. 'I am so scared,' Diana said, looking every bit of it.

'So am I, babe!' I said, putting my hands on her shoulders.

As we drove through the city, the pink that I was looking for peeped out from what looked like the older part of the city. There was a mountain range yonder, the Aravallis. Dry, barren, still standing tall in the heat. The houses were very different from anywhere else in the country; marble was predominant in the architecture. Habitation seemed to grow sparse as we crossed the city limits. Too excited to sleep despite taking an early morning flight in, Diana and I had our eyes glued to the windows. The dusty winds were giving us a warm welcome.

The cars slowed down as we drove through a massive iron gate. I shifted in my seat. Dee adjusted her clothes. I didn't know what to tell her, I was as nervous as she was. Aryaman opened the door on Dee's side and offered her his hand so she could get out. I opened my side of the door and got out before anyone could reach me. I simply could not sit inside anymore, although Aditya had already walked a few steps towards me—the sight of him was comforting enough. I placed my hand on his elbow as we walked right behind Aryaman and Dee towards the reception party standing at the massive entrance of the palace they called home.

Aryaman's mother stood at the head of the crowd. She looked at him with love that all moms in the world have in their eyes when they gaze upon their child. Dee touched her feet, along with Aryaman. She blessed them and said, 'She is prettier than you told me!' and kissed Dee's forehead. Dee was smiling, so was I. Aditya and I were introduced to her and we touched her feet to get her blessings.

'Both of you make a lovely couple,' she said. I blushed a little, not knowing what to say. 'Meera and I are not married, Auntyji, we are just friends,' said Aditya, coming to my rescue. 'I am sorry, that was presumptuous,' she said, smiling at him and then turned to me, 'I love your name, betaji. Meerabai was a Rajput princess from a kingdom not very far from here,' referring to that legendary poetess-saint, a lifelong devotee of Krishna.

'Meera is a Captain, Mom, a princess in her own right,' Aryaman interjected. I just stood there smiling from ear to ear, looking at Dee, who seemed to be feeling better with every passing minute. We were escorted into the palace after the very Rajasthani welcome of aarti, tika and a garland. The place looked like it was an old building with the most contemporary interiors. Dee and I were taken to a huge room decorated in earthy colours, by women in traditional clothes who stole glances at us. A window with a canopy on it overlooked a green lawn dotted with white garden furniture here and there. 'This is unreal,' I said, as I sat on the bed.

'Tell me about it! Bollywood kinds,' Dee replied; she was smiling.

'You are going to be queen of this palace,' I said.

'Damn! Don't say scary stuff, Em.' She threw a pillow at me. There was a knock on the door, which made us both sit up straight. We weren't used to any of it by now. 'Come in,' Dee said. I made a face at her and said, '*Andar aa jaiye* (Please come in),' loudly. The lady who came in joined her palms, bowed low from her waist and looked at us. 'Baisa, Banna requests your presence, and yours,' she said and left.

Dee stood up hurriedly and checked herself in the mirror; she looked ravishing in Indian attire. 'Shall we proceed, Your Highness?' I teased.

'I'm going to beat you, Meera, if you keep that up,' she retorted as we left the room. On a rather large chair in the middle of the room sat someone who looked like an older version of Aryaman. He was wearing a white kurta-pyjama and a black bandi-coat. Aunty sat next to him, sipping tea. Aryaman and Adi were smiling as they were in conversation with him. Aryaman stood up as soon as he saw us.

'Dad, this is Diana,' he said. Dee touched the older man's feet.

'God bless you, child,' he said, placing his hands on Dee's head, 'and who is this pretty girl?' He looked at me. I touched his feet too.

'She is Meera,' Aunty told him with a smile. 'Diana's best friend.'

'Lovely to meet you,' he said, as we took our places. Aunty poured us tea. 'You have a beautiful home,' I said.

'Thank you, betaji, this house has been in the family for about a hundred years. My great-grandfather had to fight a war to save this place. Since then the men of the family have been protecting and preserving it. The women of the family have been making this house a home, one generation after another. Now it is Diana's turn.' He and Aunty smiled. 'The festivities start tomorrow, all of you should get some rest. We have grand plans for welcoming Diana into the family,' he said as he glanced at Dee, who had a blank look on her face.

He addressed her gently, 'To make things perfect around here all you need are two things: one is love and the other is inclination. Everything will automatically fall into place. You don't have to worry at all.'

Dee smiled back at him and said 'Thank you.' For the first time in forever I saw tears well up in her eyes.

My mother arrived early next morning along with Dee's dad. We met them at the gate, the four of us together. Mom hugged me and didn't let go till she had cried and hidden her tears again. I maintained, as always, that I never cried. Aditya ruffled my hair from the other side. He then met my mother. 'Adi, mere bachche, it's been so long since I have seen you!' she exclaimed.

'I know, Aunty, I am sorry, I have been a little busy,' he replied.

'Sorry to interrupt your little reunion here, but I think I am meeting you after longer than Adi,' I said to Ma.

'Yes, betu, but it's different with Adi.' She hugged him. I stomped my feet and they laughed. Just like they had ever since I could remember.

I met Dee's dad with a hug. 'How are you, Uncle?' I asked.

'Just as I was, sweetheart; Diana told me you came down on a day's notice. You are a good friend.' He pulled my cheek.

'She would do the same for me, Uncle,' I said.

'Yes, she would if you give her a chance. So when are you and Aditya getting married?' he asked.

'It's Dee's wedding, Uncle, let's talk about her, not me please.' I dodged another bullet. Lots of introductions across generations and lots of blessings later we all got settled into the festive mode. The functions were beginning in the evening.

The three-day-long celebrations were kicked off by guns being fired in the air. Beats of the dhol reverberated in the lawn and the palace was dressed up like a bride. Folk songs could be heard in all corners of the palace. Dee sat in the middle of a huge hall filled with women, wearing the traditional Rajasthani poshak in vibrant colours and jewellery. Mehendi was applied on Dee's palms and feet. I was fluttering around like a happy butterfly, singing and dancing and showing off my lehenga! Women were singing in happy voices while they played the dholki. The maids served food in big thaals. Jaljeera and thandai made the rounds.

On the other side of the palace there was a different scene altogether. The men banned from this function, were all gathered at the other side. They had a special evening just for themselves. It was a Rajput tradition called the Manonaach. An array of meat and alcohol was being served, different kinds of songs were being played; they even had local dancers perform for them, I was told.

I had a big mind to sneak a peek at the other side; so I looked around the room to get some help. The only person I thought could perhaps help me, had her hands full with things. I walked up to her and tapped her shoulder.

'Aunty! I want to see what the Manonaach is, can I please?' I said to Aryaman's mother.

'Women aren't allowed to do that, betaji,' she said benignly. I pulled a sad face. 'Well, by rights women are not allowed to see it,' she amended, trailing a finger down my cheek, 'but if someone told you of a secret room that had a peephole....'

'Oh Aunty, you are the best.' I kissed her. She summoned a maid and gave her instructions: '*Chhoti Baisa ko jharokhe waale kamre main le jao* (Take Chhoti Baisa to the room with the jharokha-window).' The maid bowed and started walking; I followed her happily. We walked through a long, very spacious corridor dotted with paintings of Aryaman's ancestors probably, and elegant little chairs and sofas along the walls on either side, till we reached the room. The maid led me there, bowed and then left. I found the jharokha-window, which looked directly down into the hall a floor below. It had a net on it and so only one side could see the other. I saw women performing in groups, men drinking, most of them too busy in conversations to look at the dance. Some others ogled away. I saw Aryaman standing beside his father with a drink in his hand, having a polite conversation with someone. I was scanning the room for Aditya, and just then he opened the door and entered with a helper. 'What the freakin' hell!' he said.

'You're not supposed to see me here,' I answered severely.

'You're not supposed to be here!'

'I was just having a look, I think I better go now that I've been caught out.' I headed for the door. But luck was not with me; Aryaman's dad stepped into the room. He stopped short at the door as he saw me there, and then he looked at Aditya. Both of us were deeply embarrassed and so we said nothing. 'I have a hidden stash of cuban cigars in this room, I am just going to take those and leave.' He almost giggled.

'Uncle, I ...umm, I just wanted to see what Manonaach was,' I stammered.

'Don't apologize, sweetheart, I was once your age. Aditya is a fine choice.' He winked at me.

'But Un...uncle.' I didn't know what to say.

'I won't tell, if you won't tell.' He waggled the pack of cigars at me and walked out of the room.

I looked at Aditya, who was still in disbelief. 'I think I should go now,' I said to him.

'I think so too. You know what else I think? I think you look very pretty, Meera, and also I think you are insane. Now go.' He smiled and I ran out.

That night, back in our room, Diana and I both slept with a smile on our faces. The next morning was beautiful, a dawn like never before. My best friend was getting married! She would also one day be the senior-most lady hierarchically, at this palace I was standing in. Cool air blew across my face as I stood at the window looking at my mother and Aryaman's mother bond over the plants in the garden. My mother looked happy, and I was happy seeing her like that.

Dee was still fast asleep, unaware of the hoopla around her. I kissed her cheek, she smiled. 'Good morning, Baisa,' I said to her, 'rise and shine!'

'Good morning, Meera, do you know how much I love you!' She hugged me tight.

'I know,' I said and rolled over her. 'Now get up, we have lots to do, the baraat comes in at 20.00 hours. You need to be ready before that!'

'Aye aye, Captain,' she said.

That was the last conversation that Dee and I could have in the entire day. From her haldi to coordinating with the makeup artist who was coming in to get her dressed for the evening, I was running around all over the place.

Aditya was doing the same for Aryaman. We crossed paths multiple times in the day, but all we could do was trade smiles. His 'I think you look pretty' was still ringing in my ears.

The haldi ceremony was being held in our wing of the palace; a wing that had been designated as the bride's wing and housed all her people—all four of us: Dee's dad, Adi, Mom and me! The bulk of the women adorning the haldi ceremony were thus from Aryaman's side, dressed in their traditional best.

A combination of herbs and turmeric was being applied onto Dee's arms by the elderly ladies. My mother sat right beside her. The songs were different from those that were sung during the mehendi. I was standing in a corner, making things available to whoever asked for them; I was doing my maid-of-honour duties. Soon after the ceremony was over Diana would dress for the evening. As soon as the colourful crowd was led into the dining area by my mother, I introduced the make-up team to Diana, who did not seem very happy with the idea of four people working on her at the same time.

'I don't need so many of them,' she told me plaintively. So much for working with a fashion mag! 'Yes, you do,' I replied sternly.

'But why?'

'Because I said so!' I answered and gave her a look.

Reluctantly she walked into the designated room with the team in tow. I left her and went to get dressed. The red light on my phone was blinking; there was a message from Aryaman: *'Thank you so much, Captain, I owe you big. Don't leave her side, and tell her I love her. Also, I love you.'*

My fingers flew over the keys as I typed: *'I will stand by her, till you come and take her away. I love you too, Captain, but if you even think of hurting my friend, I will kill you, I promise.'*

That's all I needed to rejuvenate myself. I picked up my clothes for the evening and walked back to where Dee was. I entered the room and noticed the transformation. She looked every bit a queen. Beautiful as a picture. I stood there looking at her. She hugged me when she saw me standing there.

'You are going to spoil your makeup,' I told her while she held on to me.

'Do you think that is going to stop me from hugging you?' she replied.

'Okay, now don't get all emotional on me, Dee, I am sad enough that I have to share you with a man now,' I said, making the air lighter.

'Very funny, Meera. I am here because you asked me to take the leap of faith. I did, and now I am glad I did,' she said.

'I am glad you did too, love,' I said and hugged her again.

'Now before your knight in shining armour comes knocking, let's get dressed,' I said briskly.

✈

The baraat could be heard from kilometres away. There were twenty dhols playing in sync, I was told later. People were firing bullets in the air. It was like a king had won a war and was now coming to claim his lover. Aryaman was driven up in a vintage Rolls Royce, with Aditya sitting beside him. That sight made my heart skip a beat. The parents and other close relatives and friends of the groom's family followed in a long procession of vintage cars.

The groom got off, unsheathed his ceremonial sword and touched it to the top of the doorway. My beaming mother welcomed him with an aarti, he touched her feet and entered. Aditya walked right behind him; the jodhpuris they had picked for themselves were stunning.

The rest of what happened felt like a dream. Dee, the blushing bride, walked around the fire hand in hand with her prince, taking the seven vows of standing by each other always. There was a little chill in the wind. Everything around was surreal. My cheeks were hurting from all the smiling and wayward tears were taking their chance, trickling down without warning.

Aditya was sitting next to me, with the reflection of the fire on his face. It was all so perfect. In that moment, everything else was forgotten. He caught me staring at him, I looked away quickly. He put his hand across my shoulder, 'Do you want something, Meera?' he asked. I shook my head. 'Who would have thought …' he trailed off.

'That Dee would get married before any of us?' I questioned.

'That you could look so beautiful…your eyes, Meera, I can see stars in them.' He held my gaze without blinking.

I didn't want to blink either, but I had to break the trance; so I looked towards Dee and Aryaman, who were now taking everybody's blessings. I looked up at the sky, the moon looked like it was dancing upon the smoke that was rising from the palace grounds. On that starry night, my friend who never believed in fairy tales became a part of one.

A New Day Dawns

The last and final day of celebrations had arrived. For the first time since I had landed in India I had slept without my roomie, Dee. I was woken up by the maid knocking at my door. She was carrying the clothes that I was to wear for the day's ceremonies. Dee had picked a peach-coloured sari for me since it was a morning event. This was also the longest time I had been seen adorning Indian attire in the last decade.

My phone was buzzing all the while I tried to catch my last five minutes of sleep. I answered it. 'Good morning, madam, I am Chhaya, the junior make-up artist. Kalpana madam wants to know when she can start working on Diana madam,' she said in a shrill voice.

'I shall call you back in ten minutes, please ask your madam to be ready by then,' I replied and jumped out of bed. I looked at my watch, it was 10 a.m. The function was supposed to begin in an hour, and there was too much to be done. I had to get Dee sorted for the event, also dress up and be there on time to help. I texted Dee and sat back waiting for her reply. Five minutes and no response. I had no option but to run across the palace to the other wing, look for Aryaman's room and wake them up. That was something I so wasn't looking forward to doing, plus I didn't even have time to change.

I could see people were already dressed. I was still in my PJs and Snoopy as the Red Baron tee from the night before. My hair was all over the place, unkempt as ever. Even with all the colourful clothes and decorations, I stood out like a sore thumb. The maids and servants I passed while running, gave me polite stares. I reached the groom's side of the palace and began to walk. I could see Aryaman's dad sitting on a swing, sipping tea while he read the morning papers. I tied my hair in a bun and walked towards him.

'Good morning, Uncle,' I said.

'Good morning, sweetheart. Looks like you slept well,' he said, smiling.

'I did, Uncle, but I could have done with five minutes more of sleep.' I giggled.

'That's all that is needed always, five minutes more.' He laughed and sipped his tea. 'Why are you up then, I say you should go get those five minutes, betaji.'

'I need to find Diana, get her started with the preparations for the function. Isn't it supposed to begin in a bit?' I asked, now curious about his laidback attitude.

'It is! I am helping your aunty by sitting here. All she wanted me to do was stay out of her way.' He was laughing.

'You are awesome, Uncle,' I said to him, 'now please tell me the way to Aryaman's room so I can do my duty.'

'Go up those stairs, the first door to your right is where you should find them,' he said, pointing to the stairs.

'Thank you, and see you soon,' I said and ran again.

✈

I knocked at the door feebly once, Aryaman opened it almost immediately which caught me by surprise.

'Hi!' I said, feeling like an idiot.

'Hi back!' he replied, smiling.

'I need to talk to Diana.' I was a little awkward.

'You can talk to me too, you know, Captain. If I remember right, till last night we were good friends.' He chuckled.

'We still are, Aryaman, this is just a little weird. I mean I didn't want to be the one waking you up so early after your wedding night and all that,' I replied, smiling shyly.

'Oh, like that.' He rolled his eyes, 'Wait until you get married to know the secret of the wedding night, my friend.' He patted my shoulder.

'You can come inside, Em, Diana is right here. I was on my way out to see Dad anyway,' he said and walked out.

'Will see you soon.' I waved as he left and I entered the room. Diana was sitting at the coffee table next to the wall of glass which overlooked the garden. She looked ravishing even when she had just woken up.

'Good morning, Baisa,' I teased as I walked towards her.

'Em! What are you doing up so early!' she replied excitedly as she jumped up to hug me.

'I am on maid-of-honour duty, madam, you are supposed to be getting dressed for whatever it is we are doing this afternoon and I am supposed to get that done,' I replied, my arms akimbo as I shook my head.

'Drama queen!' she said, pinching my cheeks.

'Let's call Kalpana to come see me here now. I am good to go in five,' she said.

'Jo hokum, as you wish, Baisa,' I teased again and made the arrangements as per her instructions. 'What an amazing evening it was. Everything was just perfect. Just that...I missed you last night.' I winked.

'I did too,' she replied, smiling. 'I saw you sitting with Aditya throughout the evening. Both of you looked nice.'

'I know!' I replied coyly.

'Just, "I know" and not "shut up, Diana, you are crazy talking like that?"' she asked, raising her eyebrows.

'Shut up, Diana. By the way, I met Aryaman at the door, he asked me to ask you the secret of the wedding night,' I said, sounding as convincing as I could and changing the topic.

'Oh did he now!' She patted my knee as I sat across from her.

'Tell me, Dee, you have to. As your best friend I have the right to know,' I insisted.

'You won't like it.' She giggled.

'I don't care, tell me,' I pushed.

'The secret of the wedding night is that everyone is so exhausted by the endless ceremonies and partying that they end up falling asleep,' she replied.

'What does that mean?' I was curious.

'Wait for your turn and you'll see. Unless of course you elope, then you won't be so dead on your feet.' She laughed.

'Get dressed and call me.' I waved bye and walked to the door. 'And remember, Lady Diana, this discussion isn't over!'

The function scheduled for the afternoon was an array of games for the bride and the groom to play. There was also the age-old ceremony of 'mooh dikhayi', which historically meant that female relatives and wives and daughters of vassals would lift the bride's veil—which fell down to her chest—for the first time and leave a token of blessing and good wishes in her hands. The modern form of it was a more fun version of introductions.

Owing to all the prancing around in the morning, I was late in getting dressed. My phone was continuously ringing while I struggled with the sari. I saw Aditya's name flash across the screen. I dropped whatever I was doing, and answered it. 'Where are you Meera? Diana has already asked for you twice,' he said.

'I will be there in five minutes. Flying a plane is easier than tying a sari,' I said in exasperation.

'Should I send someone to help you?' he asked.

'Please don't, let everyone be with Dee, I shall manage,' I answered and hung up.

A minute later, Aditya strode in shutting the door behind him. I was so surprised to see him that I held the half-tied sari in my hand and stopped midway.

'Just put your hands up and stand straight,' he commanded, taking the sari from me. I did exactly as I was told to do. He moved around me once, then he made the pleats and signalled to me to tuck them in. After I followed his instructions correctly, he lowered my arms and draped the pallu over my left shoulder and told me to pin it there. ''

I fidgeted with that for a second and it was done.

'See you there in two minutes,' he said as he walked out of the door. I stood there looking at myself in the mirror. I saw a smile plastered across my face that wouldn't go away. I had seen that before. I brushed my hair, wore the earrings kept on the table, still smiling. Then I picked up my phone and walked out towards the hall.

It was a huge gathering. Smiling faces filled the hall. Diana and Aryaman were fishing for a ring in a large bowl of milk. The first one to pull it out would have the upper hand! There were always a bunch of games played after any traditional Indian wedding. The games stemmed from the era of child marriages. The little bride and marginally older groom would most probably have been very tired and grumpy by the end of everything, and liable to either squabble or cry; the games would have provided a diversion, until they could be carted back for a nap. These days, they served to provide no end of amusement for onlookers; less so for the happy couple.

I saw my mother sitting right next to Diana. Her dad was also close by. Aryaman's side of the family was cheering for him to win. Dee looked up as if to search for me. She made eye contact with Aditya, who pointed in my direction. She looked at me, smiled in contentment and signalled for me to come closer. As I tried to make way through the crowd I heard a familiar voice scream my name.

'Meera didi!' I heard Rhea say as I turned around and saw her walking towards me.

'Hey Rhea! You look like a pretty little lady,' I said as I hugged her.

'Talking about pretty, you look as beautiful as you always have,' she said sweetly.

'It's so nice to see you after such a long time, kiddo,' I said to her.

'Likewise, MD, I was excited the moment Bhai told me that you were coming,' she said excitedly as she waved to all the four faces she knew in the crowd.

'You should have come day before yesterday, stayed with us and attended the wedding,' I said.

'My plans changed because Ahana was supposed to fly down with me, and she did not want to come here for that long,' she said, still smiling. By this time Aditya had noticed Rhea and was making his way towards us.

'Ahana, who? Is she a friend of yours?' I asked.

'Ahana is Bhai's would-be fiancée,' she answered as she looked around. 'She was right behind me when we entered.'

Just then I noticed Aditya hugging a very pretty girl awkwardly. I pointed to her and asked Rhea, 'Is that her?'

'That is her,' she replied. 'Come here, I want to introduce you to her, please,' she tugged my hand. I walked behind her; as we reached them Aryaman's mother called out to me. 'Meera betaji, we need to start with the mooh dikhayi soon after this game is over. Will you oversee the arrangements?'. I just nodded, taking account of the thoughts running at supersonic speed in my head.

'Ahana, this is Meera didi,' Rhea said, her voice bursting with pride. 'She is the one I was telling you about.'

'Meera, this is Ahana, Mathur uncle's daughter.' Aditya completed the introduction.

'Hello Meera,' she said to me, 'I have heard so much about you, it's nice to finally meet you.'

She reached out her hand to shake mine. I hugged her instead of shaking hands. 'It's nice to meet you too.' She smiled, Rhea also smiled. Relief ran across Aditya's face, just before he smiled too. He asked Rhea to take Ahana to meet my mother and Diana before the next function started. When they were gone, it was just Aditya and I, with an awkward silence between us. 'Sweet girl,' I said, shattering the silence.

'Yes. I have been spending some time with her in the last month. Mom and Dad really like her,' he answered.

'I like her too, she is pretty and smart from what I gather,' I said as I looked at her meet my people.

'They want us to get engaged next month,' he replied in a tone that did not complement his words.

'That is awesome news, Adi,' I said as I hugged him. He did not hug me back this time.

I joined the womenfolk where Diana's mooh dikhayi ceremony was about to begin. Diana waved to me as I entered the room. 'Did you meet her too?' she whispered in my ear as I stood beside her.

'Yes, I did,' I answered.

'I don't like her,' she said, still whispering.

'Why not, Dee, she is nice to look at, carries herself well, like a lady, she is so unlike me,' I replied.

'That is exactly why I don't like her.' She looked at me and grimaced. 'There is something wrong about her.'

'As far as I am concerned, she is Adi's choice. That cannot be wrong,' I said.

'She isn't Adi's choice, Em. We all know that!' Dee exclaimed in annoyance.

'Not the time or the place to talk about that. And anyway, a lot of water has passed under that particular bridge,' I replied sternly.

The ladies had gathered around us and were making their way towards Diana, each blessing her, feeding her sweets and giving her an envelope with a token of blessing in it. I was standing beside her, taking the envelopes from her hand, and smiling at the women who force-fed her.

Dee pulled me close and hissed, 'I will puke on my Manish Malhotra sari in public if I am fed another barfi. Do something Em.' I tapped her shoulder, signalling her to hold her horses.

I summoned a maid who was serving dry fruits to the guests, handed her the plate of sweets and swiped her plate of dry fruit. Dee sqeezed my hand and whispered, 'I love you.'

✈

The crowd withered as the food was served. Also, the men were allowed back into the premises. Aryaman walked straight up to his bride. 'How are we doing?' he asked.

'Not bad at all,' she replied.

'Don't mind me, but unlike you two, I cannot fill my stomach with love; so I shall go get some food,' I teased, taking the first chance of getting out of there. Aditya was introducing Ahana to the people around. They walked arm in arm as they met people. I almost bumped into Aryaman's dad as I walked out of the hall, since I was looking elsewhere at Ahana and Aditya. He followed the direction of my gaze, narrowed his eyes at what he saw and asked, 'Who is she?'

'She is Aditya's would-be fiancée,' I replied, smiling at him.

'I see,' he said.

'Cute, no?' I asked in a childlike voice.

'Yes, very!' he said as he pinched my cheek. I walked out to the food counter to fill my plate. I had put on it enough food for Dee, Aryaman, Aditya and me, when I realized that Adi wouldn't be eating with us this time. Also it was then that I saw Ahana filling a plate with food, just behind me. We exchanged smiles. She walked up to me.

'Aditya tells me you guys are childhood friends?' she said.

'Yes,' I replied.

'So you know all about him,' she continued, 'I haven't known him for that long, so this is all a little scary for me.'

'Aditya is a great guy, you don't have to be scared at all,' I replied.

'Dating is okay, but getting married is a whole different thing,' she said.

'Ahana, Aditya is one person who makes everything easy for you. If he has decided to get married to you, then he must have given it a lot of thought,' I said reassuringly.

'But he isn't in love with me,' she said plaintively.

'I think that takes some time.' My throat was parched and I had to gulp before I could sound normal.

'How will I know it's time?' she continued, her expressions not changing at all.

'When he is in love, there is no one like Adi. So you will know. He will make sure you have heaven under your feet. No one does it better than him. Aditya's love knows no boundaries, he knows love best. So don't worry!' I replied in one breath.

'If he is such a great guy, Meera, why don't you get married to him?' she asked.

I had no answer to her question, I did not know what to say. I knew something had to be said, or this moment would raise a lot of questions. After what was perhaps the longest minute ever, I said, 'Some things are just not meant to be.'

Sleepless in Manila

The departure from Jaipur was chaotic: all of us were leaving at the same time. My mother and Dee's dad were going back to Mumbai, as were Rhea, Ahana and Aditya. Aryaman and Dee were leaving for London for their European honeymoon. And I was going back to Manila almost at the same time too. We were dropped off at the airport by Bhanwar Singhji and his convoy of men. There were so many of us together, that Jaipur Airport looked like it belonged to us.

Aryaman's parents came along to see us off. They met everyone, blessed them and also handed them shiny envelopes with money in them, in keeping with the Rajput tradition. I stood beside my mother who was showing the first signs of getting emotional. Aryaman's dad walked up to me, I bent to touch his feet but he stopped me. 'You are the daughter that we never had, Meera,' he said. I just smiled, since anything I said could not come close to what he had just said.

'He always wanted a daughter, now he has two,' Aryaman's mother joined in, 'Dee and you. You are family now.'

'Thank you so much, Auntyji,' I replied. 'I am so glad we met, I hope to see you very soon.'

Aunty hugged my mother; they had a long conversation about the festivities, keeping in touch and gardening amongst other things. I moved a little away to text Ding about my arrival. When I was done I saw that everyone was busy, Aryaman and Dee were discussing something, Rhea was keeping Ahana entertained, and Aditya was talking on the phone. So I kept fidgeting with my phone and waited for them to announce my flight.

The only person who wasn't busy walked up to me. 'Are you happy you are leaving, or are you sad?' Aryaman's dad asked.

'I am sad that I am leaving your kingdom, but I am happy that I am going back to mine,' I replied.

'I like that.' He chuckled. 'When are you inviting us over to your kingdom for another round of celebrations?' he asked me.

'You can come over any time, Uncle, and we shall celebrate with cuban cigars!' I dodged.

'I am a champion at the game you are playing,' he said pinching my cheek 'I know, you know exactly what I am asking about.'

'I have had one answer for all questions in that area, I'd rather be flying!' I grinned.

'When I was young, I had a huge crush on this blonde lady. She looked pretty as an angel, also spoke like one. She once said, "A career is wonderful, but you can't curl up with it on a cold night,"' he stated. I looked at him with confusion in my eyes. 'Marilyn Monroe, my love.' His eyes twinkled. 'It made sense to me; I hope it does to you too.' He patted my shoulder.

My flight was announced. After a protracted session of goodbyes with Rhea, hugs from Dee and Aryaman, I walked towards the gate. My mother was walking with me as always till the very end. 'We haven't had time to catch up on this trip,' she complained.

'Yes, Mom, but I shall be back very soon,' I replied.

'Take care of yourself, eat right, make sure you have green vegetables in your daily meal. Drink a lot of water,' she went on.

'Mother India, I know this checklist by heart now.' My arms went around her. 'Now, if it's okay with you, dear Mom, may I board the flight? They seem to be waiting for me.'

She nodded. I walked away. I hadn't had a chance to say goodbye to Aditya since he was on a work call. I turned around from the gate and our eyes met. I waved to him; he smiled and waved back.

Nine hours later we finally landed hard on to the tarmac in Manila, I had just woken up, very groggy after sleeping all the way on the flight. I could hear the cabin crew announcements. Even with the PA on I could hear a voice in my head mumbling like it was a dream or something. I tried hard to listen to it: for some strange reason 'some things are just not meant to be' was playing in a loop in my head.

The first thing I did after I sat in the car was call scheduling. I wanted to fly—more like needed to do it. Distance between the earth and me made me comfortable. It was seven in the morning, shifts were just changing. People were waking up to a bright sunny day in Manila.

'How was the wedding, Captain madam?' Ding asked. Since I had sent him a text with the flight details, I had known for sure that he would be there. No one understood duty better than Ding. 'It was very nice, I had lots of fun, but I am happy to be back,' I replied honestly.

The manager from scheduling called to tell me that they

hadn't taken any booking for the next two days, since they were not expecting me back so early. He also told me that Captain Garcia was in Singapore with Jenny and the kids for a vacation. I asked him to let me know if anything came up. Then I sent a text to Captain G: '*I am back in town, missed Nefertiti and you too. You a little more maybe. Tell me when you land back.*'

He called the moment he received it. 'Hey kiddo, you are back earlier than I thought,' he said.

'I did not go back and spend time in Mumbai on the way back as planned earlier. Flew back directly from the wedding,' I replied.

'I am surprised, but it's nice to have you back,' he said.

'When do you get back?' I asked.

'Late tomorrow night; till then catch up on the rest, we shall be flying a lot more than we did, since the weather is better now,' he said.

'I shall, sir, say hello to Jenny, and have fun,' I said.

'I will; oh, and did you get me those round, orange sweet things from India?' he asked.

'Yes sir, I got you two kilos of jalebi, happy?'

'Good girl,' he said and hung up. I had nothing to do at the apartment, so I asked Ding to take me to the hangar. The maintenance guys were always around. I would only learn something if I hung around.

They were more than happy to see me there. We had bonded over all the months I had spent with the company, and also at the parties Captain G threw for us. They were doing routine checks on all the aircrafts in the hanger.

There was a Cessna Citation CJ2, a Super King Air B-200, a Pilatus PC-12 and also a Super King Air C-90 which is what

Nefertiti was. There were three helicopters parked on the ramp too, which were to be checked later in the day.

I changed into the jumpsuit that Ding got me from the company office, tied my hair and became a part of the surroundings. Till a coffee break was called I was under my aircraft checking the suspension on the main landing gear. The ground crew around was amused and amazed looking at me do that. For most part of the day I worked as the chief's assistant, trying to understand everything he said and did. These were things that flying school hadn't taught me.

After he was done with my aircraft the chief was going to do an engine run of the Bell 407, a four-blade, single-engine helicopter. It was used a lot in rescue operations and also in civil transport services. I could never trust helicopters much; probably it was their non-aerodynamic shape that scared me. Or maybe it was the rotor on the top that did. I had never even been inside one of those machines, let alone fly them.

The chief asked me if I wanted to do the engine run with him. I agreed to it only for the thrill of it, knowing very well that we wouldn't leave ground. I sat on the co-pilot's seat, while he went through his checklist. He signalled for me to put on the headphones, and spoke to ground control asking them permission to start engines for the check. Clearances received and confirmations given, the engine roared to life and the rotor went crazy. The noise was much louder than it is on an aircraft. I felt like I was sitting on the engine in a dome. 'I used to fly one of these when I was younger,' the chief said, 'then I met with an accident, broke my back, and now I cannot fly anymore, but I love to be around them. This is my life.'

'You are a star,' I said and saluted him.

He smiled and turned the engine off. He made calls to

ground control again. I got out of the helicopter, walked a few steps away and looked back at it. 'You are not as bad as I thought you would be; someday soon, we shall meet again,' I whispered to it.

It was almost evening when I left the hangar. Ding drove me back to the apartment. Everything was exactly like I had left it. There was a sense of calm around the place. Ordering in as always was the option I chose. I planned on changing the pizza order but ended up ordering the exact same one, for the hundredth time. Though travel fatigue was catching up on me, I was tired, not sleepy. The lights were off, the curtains drawn, the room was as dark as I liked it, but sleep was nowhere around. I lay on the bed with my eyes tightly shut, trying very hard to sleep. After a while I realized I was gazing blankly at the ceiling, a conscious effort was needed to shut my eyes. I tried doing that for some time and then gave up, got out of bed, turned on the lights, and started unpacking my bag.

I put the clothes that needed to be washed into the machine, folded and arranged the rest in the closet, set aside my maid-of-honour dress for dry-cleaning. Next I unpacked my shoes, cleaned them and arranged them in the rack. Then I worked similarly on the books that I ended up collecting on the journey. Still there was no sign of sleep. I glanced at my watch, it was 2.30 a.m. I decided to do the drill one more time. So I turned off the light and drew the shades one more time. This time I also added my iPod to the scene, turned it on, put the earphones on the pillow and shut my eyes.

I woke up at 6 a.m., without the alarm sounding. My iPod lay battery drained, next to me. I picked it up and set it out to charge, freshened up, changed into running shorts and a tee. I had to wait until the iPod had enough battery to last for the run, so I turned on the washing machine, picked the newspaper from outside my door, made a list of stuff I needed replenished in the fridge on a sticky note and stuck it on the fridge for housekeeping to see. Then I wore my shoes, stuffed some cash into my socks, picked up the iPod and shut the door behind me. The concierge wasn't at his desk when I crossed it. He was standing outside with the guards, enjoying his morning coffee. They smiled at me as I appeared at the gate.

The wind blew onto my face while I stood there for a second, trying to decide which direction to go in. I moved from the building towards the sea; I just had to cross the road and there it was. Once I was there, I took a deep breath and ran. There were too many things that crossed my mind while I was running. The whole trip in bits and pieces, Dee's face filled with joy, Aryaman's eyes showing pride, the grandeur of the palace, the madness during the Manonaach, Aunty calling me 'betaji', my mother's hug when she met me, Rhea's effervescence.

The conversation that I had with Aryaman's dad at the airport was fresh in my mind. The presence of a father figure was never missed in my life since my mother was also the best dad in the world, but that moment I shared with uncle was different. I also remembered everything about Aditya in the minutest of detail. The way he looked at me at Mumbai Airport when they came to receive me, his non-stop chatter with Aryaman, his look when he saw me in the store room, the effect that light from the fire had on his face, the moment when he walked into my room to help me with the sari, the final moment when our eyes met at the airport. I remembered everything.

Suddenly I stopped running, I was out of breath. That's when I realized that I had run about eight kilometres and was at the other end of the boulevard. I also realized that I was running faster than I usually did and my heart was beating like it was going to explode.

I found a bench and sat on it while my breathing became normal. I put my hands over my eyes for an instant, and I could see Aditya and Ahana walking arm in arm meeting people. Aditya's words rang in my ears, 'They want us to get engaged next month.' I opened my eyes, stood up and started running back to where I started from. I decided that I had to put an end to this. I had to push all these thoughts out of my head. I called Ding and asked him to pick me up as soon as possible. I was going back to the maintenance hangar for some more solace.

The Chief was working on the B-200 when I entered; he already had an intern assisting him and I didn't want to disturb him. I noticed that one of the loaders was getting ready to wash my plane. I asked him if I could do it. He was more than happy to pass on his duty to me. I climbed up on the ladder with the sponge in my hand and scrubbed every centimetre of the machine. It took me more than an hour to get it done all the way. The loader then helped me pull out a water hose. The pressure made the hose difficult to handle, but it was fun at the same time. My plane was shiny as new once I was done with her. There was something about what I had just done that calmed me down.

My post-lunch laziness was taken care of by my mother's call. 'I have not received a single "taking off" or "landed" message in the last two days,' she said.

'That is because I haven't been flying, Ma,' I replied.

'The rule is that we talk whenever you land, but that doesn't mean we cannot talk otherwise,' she complained jokingly.

'Yes, Mother,' I teased. 'Tell me, what's new?'

'Aditya might get engaged soon, I spoke to his mother. She told me that they are only waiting for him to confirm the date,' she said.

'That is very good for them,' I replied.

'I had always hoped that Aditya and you would end up together; what could be better than marrying your best friend?' she said.

'Some things are just not meant to be,' I shot back in a resigned tone. 'Now if your soap opera story is over, can I get back to work?'

'I don't watch soap operas,' she almost screamed.

'Yes, Mom! You call them serials,' I joked.

'Just let me get my hands on you this time, I'll give you such a beating that you'll never forget it,' she threatened.

'I love you, Mom.' I tried to save my skin.

'I love you too,' she replied before hanging up. It always worked.

On the way back home in the evening, I thought of giving Aditya a call to congratulate him. But then I decided to message him instead. '*Heard the good news from Mom, many congratulations on finding a great life partner,*' I wrote and hit the send button.

'Thank you! Why aren't you calling? Should I call? Are you busy?' he replied.

'Sort of, will call you when I can,' I replied.

For the first time in forever I did not feel like talking to Aditya.

Back at the Pink Pearl, it was the second night in a row that sleep deserted me. It had been a long tiring day; on a usual day like this I could have just dropped on to the bed only to wake up the next afternoon. Instead I came home, made pasta for dinner, and watched the news on TV, but sleep still eluded me.

I had slept for four hours in the last twenty-four hours. Although I was as nocturnal as one could be, this was very different from all those nights spent awake by choice. This was failure to sleep even when it was needed. My legs were hurting from the strenuous run, my hands ached from the work done at the hangar, and my head throbbed from the lack of sleep. There were so many things that were not right with me, but there was something in particular that was wrong with me, something that was making me sleepless in Manila.

The Final Approach

Captain Garcia was back from his vacation with more stories to tell. The balance in my life was restored again. The sales and scheduling department of the company were working overtime to cover for the slack during the bad weather months. We were flying more than ever.

Captain G never ran out of things to talk about. Sometimes he spoke about Jenny and himself, other times about people and places. I was mostly on the listening end of those conversations, since I spoke less than he did. He told me that he had proposed to Jenny in Singapore, and that they had set a date for the wedding. My talking had further reduced since I came back from India. He seemed to notice this too and so on one of the long flights he changed sides with me. 'Tell me all that happened at Diana's wedding?' he said.

I gave him all the details of the cities, locations, venues. I told him about the hospitality and customs that were followed, the food that was served. He smiled at the mention of food. I told him how Aryaman was a real prince and that made Dee a real princess, how the wedding procession had arrived in vintage cars. He was listening intently even as he made funny faces. I also told him that as we were leaving, Uncle had explained to me in one line that my career was a part of my life and not the other way round. He narrowed his eyes when he heard that.

Then I told him how Aditya and I had fun while prepping for the wedding and taking care of guests, how we were mistaken for a couple, and also how we dodged the 'When are you getting married?' questions.

'So when are you guys getting married?' he asked when I was done talking.

'Who? Aditya and I? Never,' I replied.

'Why not?' he asked curiously.

'Two reasons, sir. One: some people are just not meant to be together like that, and two: he is getting engaged to someone, very soon,' I replied in one breath.

'I agree that some people are not meant to be together like that, but apparently some people are.' He was grinning.

'What is apparent, sir?' I asked, now a little miffed.

'That you are not ready to agree to the fact that you screwed up. You would rather let him go and be with someone he doesn't love, than confess to him that you should have accepted his proposal when he was here,' he said with unusual force.

'I don't think I made a mistake, I think I made a choice. I chose to stay here, in the life I have worked so hard to build. I have always dreamt of being Commander of an aircraft. I wake up and come to work every day with this aim in my head,' I replied. 'Being with Aditya wasn't part of the plan.'

'Why can't you do the two together?' he questioned. I looked at him blankly.

'That would be like having the cake and eating it too.' He winked at me.

This conversation stayed with me for days after we had landed. I needed to talk to someone who could sort out this confusion brewing in my head. I needed to call Diana. The only problem in that was that she was in Europe with Aryaman, and I didn't want to disturb them. After much deliberation and a few days of fighting with myself I decided to text her after I got back from a flight. '*Hey babe, how goes the vacation?! Please call me whenever you have a minute to spare,*' I wrote. There was no point waiting for a response immediately; so I changed, parked myself on the bed with a stack of CDs trying to decide what I could watch, since I had finished watching *Prison Break*.

I opened my laptop and saw that my email was open in a window, and there was a three-hour-old ping from Aditya. I realized I hadn't disconnected the Wi-Fi since the last time I'd used it. '*Where are you, Meera? We haven't connected since you left. Please call me when you can, I have to tell you something very important,*' it said.

I stared at it for a minute, and then closed the window.

I got up, and went and sat facing the sea. The thought of what Captain G had said was jiving in my head. I was thinking whether it was really possible for me to have my cake and eat it too. If it had to happen, I would have to leave this job, go back to India and look for another one. Finding something I liked wasn't easy there. That was the reason I was here in the first place.

On the other hand I was eligible to make commander, I had also cleared all the related exams and obtained licences, but I chose to fly as a First Officer since it was Captain G who I was flying with. Going back meant I would get a chance to move ahead. But the main concern was Aditya. He had never told me in so many words that he loved me, but he had said things that meant much more. The other major concern was that he was now getting engaged to Ahana. Would it be a wise thing for me to now think of a future for us or of returning? Was I really in love with him? When had this happened? How was I so comfortable thinking about it now? Maybe I had screwed up. Maybe it was time for me to make amends, or maybe it was too late already.

I dropped my face in my hands, trying to stop thinking. In the next minute, my phone rang. 'Dee calling' it showed.

'Heya babe, how are you?' I said.

'Hey Meera, we are both good. Having fun, but we shall be returning day after tomorrow. Aryaman has been asked to return with immediate effect, there is some kind of an emergency.'

'There is some kind of an emergency here as well.' I could not stop myself anymore.

'What has happened?'

'I think I screwed up, Dee, and this time it's going to cost me almost everything I have,' I replied.

'What are you talking about, was there another crash? What is going to cost you?' She was very concerned now.

'I am talking about Aditya,' I said. 'I think I have lost him forever!'

'Lost him forever, meaning...?' She was still confused. 'Is he all right? Are you all right? What the hell are you saying Meera, make some sense!'

'Dee, listen to me. I think I am in love with Aditya,' I said and waited for her response.

'Oh okay, that's it, right?' she said.

'That's it?' I yelled, 'How is that, "that's it"?'

'You have always been in love with Aditya, Em. It's just that you've now realized it,' she said calmly.

'And you knew it all along, but you wanted me to figure it out for myself, right?' I huffed.

'I don't think you're going to like my answer, but yes! I knew it all along, just as Aryaman did, and his parents do, your mom does,' she said.

'I am glad everyone knew. Now that I know it too, what am I going to do, Dee? He is getting engaged to Ahana anytime now,' I said in a distressed tone.

'That he is,' she said wryly.

'Do you think I should tell him?' I asked.

'I don't know, Meera, that is a call that only you can take.' She sounded all grown up.

'Hmm,' I said.

'Don't stress over it, babe, it's love, not the end of the world,' Diana said, 'I have to go now, will talk to you when I reach India. Take care,' she said breezily and signed off. I said bye in a trance and hung up. It was love and it was the end of the world. I was thinking to myself what a fool I had been. Aditya had travelled all the way over to tell me that he loved me, and all I had done was make it difficult for him. I remembered how I had felt when we had gone diving, and how it had felt at the deck of the lighthouse. Before drifting off to sleep I remembered feeling amazed someone was in love with me.

I was going to tell Aditya how I felt.

I had taken my final call.

✈

The radio crackled and a familiar voice said, 'Romeo Papa Charlie One Niner Niner Two exit runway at Bravo, proceed to parking via Zulu Lima.'

Familiar words that I had heard over a thousand times … so I knew what I had to do, like clockwork. My Commander had already made the mandatory reply call to the tower while I manoeuvred the aircraft back to its parking spot. We had just returned and landed at Ninoy Aquino International Airport in Manila—the flight to the island of Cebu and back had taken us four hours. It had been uneventful except for a minor bump here and there. That was perfectly normal in this weather.

On the flight I had told Captain G what I had decided. I was going back home.

The aircraft had come to a halt and I made my call: 'Manila tower, this is the final call for Romeo Papa Charlie One Niner Niner Two, signing off for the day.' The voice at the other end responded, 'Roger that, have a good night, madam.' It had been a good night!

The next day I met Captain Garcia, Jenny and both his kids over lunch at Aristocrat, a restaurant on Roxas Boulevard. Jenny told me she was sad that I was leaving the country, but happy that I was going home. I told her how I had to go back to sort things out for myself. I also told her that I was very sad to leave a job I loved, working with someone I looked up to so much. Captain G—living up to his reputation—cut through the emotional talk with his no-nonsense comments.

He told me that he knew someone in India who owned a charter company just like this one. Apparently this friend of his was looking for someone to be Commander on his Super King Air C 90. All I had to do was clear an F-check ride, take an interview with the management and I could have the job.

The lunch stretched to coffee and the conversation continued. By the time I reached the apartment, it was already evening. I called the number Captain G had given me, to fix up an appointment for the check ride and the interview. The voice on the other side recognized me by my name. He said Captain Garcia had spoken to him about me that afternoon. He then told me that their pilot-in-command had met with an accident, and was unfit to fly, so they were in a hurry to recruit. I told him that I would be able to fly out the next day, for the check.

So here I was, booking a flight for India, the second time in a month. This time I was going back for good. I hadn't told anyone that I was coming back. Pink Pearl's housekeeping staff helped me pack stuff that had made up the warp and weft of my life for the last one year and more. Ding drove me to the airport. 'Thank you for everything, Ding,' I said.

'Thank you Captain madam, whenever you come back, I here,' he said seriously. I shook hands with him and boarded my flight out of the Philippines.

I planned to visit Captain G's friend's charter company's office immediately upon landing at Mumbai. It was located at another airport in the Juhu area. I had carried my flight bag as hand baggage since it had all that I needed for my interview—uniform, shoes, checklists, manuals, flight charts. I was carrying the Air Navigation Book along as well, just to brush up on things. After reaching the charter company's office I was scheduled to take a check ride with an examiner from the Directorate General of Civil Aviation (DGCA), the Indian aviation authority.

I had also hired a car online for the day with a driver, since I hadn't mentioned I was coming to Dee, Adi or Mom yet. My luggage could stay in the hired car while I got on with my interview and check flight.

All that taken care of, I settled down for a study-filled journey back home, but was still somewhere between thoughts and air nav pages when we landed.

The Perfect Landing

Walking out of the same airport exit that I had some days ago, felt very different. I glanced at the place where Aditya, Dee and Aryaman had been standing when they came to receive me the last time. There was a man standing there with his arms folded and a red rose in his pocket. He was waiting for someone very impatiently. I looked away to search for the driver who was supposed to be waiting for me. I saw my name written on a placard, and I waved to the man holding it. He came running in my direction to take my luggage.

'Juhu Airport,' I told him.

'Yes, madam,' he said while he stacked my bags in the trunk of the car.

'What is your name?' I asked as I took my seat in the plush air-conditioned comfort of the car.

'Shekhar, madam,' he replied and we started moving.

'We take a left under the Bisleri factory flyover, correct, Shekharji?' I asked.

'Yes, madam, have you visited Mumbai earlier?' He was curious.

'I am from Mumbai,' I answered.

Not having attended an interview in the last couple of years was making me a little nervous. I knew that being a little less confident was better than being a little too confident. We reached the airport gates and after taking permissions from Captain Sood, the co-owner of the charter company over the phone at the guard room, we were let inside. The office wasn't as plush as I had imagined. The size of the place managed to take me by surprise. I knocked on the door of Captain Sood's cabin, trying hard to hide my disappointment. 'Come in,' he said.

As I entered I saw a man who looked like he was well into his fifties. He had more white hair than black. He wore a crisp white shirt and beige trousers. He stood up to shake my hand.

'Hello sir, I am Captain Meera Khanna,' I said.

'You look much younger than you sound,' he said, smiling gently.

I returned a polite smile.

'Captain Garcia is all praise for you; he told me you have been working with him for almost two years. He also told me you are good at your job.' He was looking at me through the glasses he had just slipped on to his nose.

'I joined their company soon after I got my licenses, and I have been with them since,' I replied.

'Why are you leaving them now?' he asked.

'I have lived away for quite a while now, it's time I came back to the motherland.' I smiled.

'Great! His loss is our gain then.' He was smiling too. 'I do not believe I need to ask you anything much, Captain. I have gone through the link of your log book that you mailed me, you seem to make the cut as far as the numbers go,' he said, 'but I shall still ask you one question.' He looked up at me again. I nodded.

'What do you think is a perfect landing?' he asked.

'The definition of that has changed for me over the years. When I got my first solo, I flared the plane 30 feet above the ground. It hit the runway with a bang and I was glad to get out of it alive... It was a perfect landing for me then!' I smiled as I answered him.

The man across the table had a poker face but his eyes were almost smiling.

'Now after so many hours of flying, I am still chasing the elusive perfect landing. Where the rear gear glides on to the tarmac like a hot knife on butter and the nose gear slides into place soon after,' I said.

'A perfect landing is a mirage—the more you want it, the more it eludes you,' he said, 'so experience required for the job, check; passion for flying, check; now all you need to do is clear the check-ride, and we can have your appointment letter printed.'

I changed into my uniform, walked to the aircraft and did my pre-flight check on an aircraft that was painted silver and red; her registration number was VT-DBI. My interviewer walked out wearing his uniform and holding a folder in his hands. 'I have given so many hours to flying these aircraft that I am now a certified examiner on them,' he said with a smile.

Flying with someone takes a lot of trust, the coordination takes time to build. Captain Sood was doing his duty and mine while I got comfortable with the cockpit. We were already holding short of the runway, while we waited for our turn to take off. He asked me if I was okay by signalling with his hand, and I gave him a thumbs-up to that. The aircraft that had kept us waiting finally landed and it was our turn to go. We were just waiting for the tower to give us the clearance. The radio crackled just as he signalled for me to take the radio. 'Victor Tango Delta Bravo India cleared for take-off,' a voice said.

'Roger that,' I replied.

Then I pushed in the throttle and manoeuvred the aircraft to the centre of the runway. I set it such that she would roll on the yellow line and gave her the power. Then—like I had done every time since the engine failure—I kissed my hand and planted it on the panel in front of me. I was in my element now. Nothing bothered me here. We did a circuit as per Captain Sood's flight plan, and were back and parked in the next ninety minutes. There were no issues that could worry me. I shook hands with Captain Sood when I was ready to leave.

'Meera, leave us your local address, someone from the head office will deliver the documents to you,' he said.

'I shall leave it at the reception, sir,' I replied, now realizing that where we were sitting was only the airport office of the charter company. I walked out and called Captain G. 'It's done,' I said. 'It wasn't as long as I had expected.'

'A check ride should always be like a skirt, short enough to be interesting but still long enough to cover everything,' he said and laughed.

'Captain Sood said he will let me know,' I said.

'Good, what are you going to do now?' he asked.

'I don't know, no flight plans made, I will just take it as it comes,' I answered. 'Will keep you posted, sir.'

'You do that kiddo, see you!' He hung up.

I got to the car parked outside the airport, sat inside, and realized I hadn't decided where to go next. I could go home, meet Mom, explain to her why I was there so suddenly, discuss with her how and what I had to do. I could call Dee, meet up with her and discuss the possibilities, but I was tired, fatigue was catching up with me. I decided that I would go to my mother's place which was in the suburbs. 'Versova, Shekharji,' I instructed the driver.

He started the car promptly. As we drove along I realized that Mumbai hadn't changed at all since I had left it. Only the amount of cars on its roads had grown in number. I knew this place so well that I had a fair idea of the places we could be stuck in traffic. I knew that we would reach my mother's in about thirty minutes from our present location.

I was looking outside the window, trying to map the changes around me. The red light on my phone caught my eye. It was a text from Aditya. 'It was nice of you to call the other night, I have been meaning to talk to you. Have to tell you something, ping back when free,' it read. He had been saying that in every conversation we had had so far, and it was not sounding good now. In fact this time it was making me breathless. I wanted to tell him what I had been thinking and going through, before he told me anything more. I wanted to scream it out loud that I was in love with him and I wanted to do it now.

'Shekharji, to Nariman Point please,' I said.

'That is in town, madam, it will take us two hours to reach,' he replied, surprised.

'I know, just turn the car around,' I replied. It took us more than an hour to reach Marine Drive from Juhu. Now that the car was being parked at Aditya's office, I realized I didn't know what I was going to do.

I entered the building, and walked to the reception. 'Where can I find Mr Aditya Kapoor's cabin?' I asked the lady behind the desk. 'Do you have an appointment, ma'am?' she asked me with a surprised smile on her face.

'I am a friend, he doesn't know I am visiting him, it would be nice if you could just tell me where to find him,' I said as I realized that she was staring at my uniform.

'His cabin is on the eleventh floor, the last door on your left,' she said.

'Thank you,' I said as I walked towards the elevators. As I got into the elevator I thought about what I was going to say, and how he would react. By the time I decided that it was pointless thinking about it, I was already standing in front of a door which had 'Aditya Kapoor' embossed on it. I took a deep breath and opened the door. I saw him sitting there, working on his laptop. My legs felt like they couldn't take my weight anymore. Blood from my brain was draining fast, making me dizzy. He hadn't seen me yet, so I called out to him. 'Adi...' I said.

'What the freakin' hell...Meera, what are you... How are you... What the hell,' he stammered as he stood up.

'Hi!' I managed.

'Hi! What a surprise, I have been trying to get in touch with you, no wonder you weren't answering the IMs,' he said. 'What are you doing here? You are in uniform, did you get the aircraft here? Why didn't you tell me?' he went on.

'One at a time, sweetheart,' I replied and smiled just like he had when he had surprised me in Subic. 'I will tell you why I am here, but you won't believe me,' I said. His face was now a combination of confusion, surprise and anticipation. 'I am here because I missed you. I am here because I would rather be here with you than anywhere else in the whole world,' I said. 'You have always been special to me, but it's only now that I realize that you are a part of me that is most important. I am here to tell you this.' I looked straight into his eyes as I spoke. He just stood there like he was frozen in the moment.

'I know you have moved on from the last time this statement was made, I know you are getting engaged to Ahana, I know that saying all this now doesn't make sense, but I also know that if I hadn't said it, it would have taken the life out of me!' I couldn't talk anymore. He walked up to me and took me into his arms. I could not make out what it meant; so I just buried my face in his chest and stayed that way for a long time. He hadn't said a word. The silence was ringing in my ears. 'I think I should leave now,' I mumbled.

'Do you have someone to take you back?' he asked.

'I do,' I replied blankly.

'I will talk to you the moment I get free from here,' he said. I nodded.

I left the building feeling as blank as I had when I entered it. I was having the longest day so far, two hours of time difference to add to it. I wanted to crash on a bed and not wake up till everything around me was back to being perfect. I called Diana.

'Heya Em,' she said chirpily.

'Hey Dee, I am in Mumbai, heading to your house, see me there when you are done with work, please,' I said.

'Wow! That's the best thing I have heard all day. I will be home in an hour, the maid is there, get something to eat and rest, you sound horrible,' she exclaimed.

'I feel horrible,' I replied.

'I will see you at home,' she said.

I was well fed as usual by Dee's maid. I showered, changed and was fast asleep by the time she came home. I woke up confused, my room was dark. It took me a second to recollect where I was. I checked the time on my phone. It was a little past midnight. I walked out to find where Diana was. Saint Cupid ambled towards me as I entered the hall. I patted his head and rubbed his neck. He was standing right in front of me, blocking my way. I sat down on the floor where I was standing, so that I could pamper him all he wanted.

'Get here already!' Dee screamed.

I got up and walked to the couch she was sitting on. She hugged me as she always did. 'Why did you wake up, you look like you could use some more rest!' she said as we sat huddled together.

'I have to tell you so many things, don't know where to start,' I said as I placed my head on her shoulder.

'Start at the beginning and tell me everything,' she ruffled my hair.

I told her all that had happened in the last twenty-four hours. She did not say anything till I was done. Her face showed happiness when I told her about the interview, anxiety when I told her about the check ride and surprise when I told her what happened at Aditya's office. She was fidgeting with her phone all the while I spoke.

'I don't know what he must be thinking after all that I said,' I said after a pause.

'I don't know that either, all I know is I am so happy that you are back for good, and so amazed at what you have done Em,' she said. 'What made you decide you wanted to tell him like that?' she asked curiously.

'He kept saying he had something important to tell me, I knew it had to do something with his engagement date. I didn't have the courage to hear what he had to say, so I had to do it

Dee, confessing love is more difficult when a girl does it, but a girl's got to do what she's got to do!' I smiled.

'I am glad you did what you did!' She was still fidgeting with her phone. I assumed it was Aryaman she was texting. I could not complain. I was sharing my best friend with another man now. 'Do you want to drive to Carter?' she asked. 'Let's go sit on our favourite bench for some time, things might just look better from there.'

'I really don't mind,' I said. The idea of the sea breeze and the sound of waves was very appealing. Ten minutes later we were driving down to our favourite haunt in the city. We had grown up visiting that place. Not as much in age, as in life. The roads were relatively empty, the night had its privileges. We stopped at Mount Mary to light a candle. It felt as serene as it always did. I could see that nothing had changed on the Bandstand, except that it had become a little cleaner. We reached Carter Road, parked our car a few feet away from the bench that we called ours and got out of the car. 'Do you want to walk?' I asked.

'Not really, I'd rather just sit,' she replied. We sat there in silence for a minute. Then Diana couldn't bear not talking anymore so she started telling me about her vacation with Aryaman in Europe. She told me that although she had always stayed alone, she now missed his presence in the house when he was gone. The phone was a lifesaver, she said. I kept smiling all through the conversation. 'It's just so nice to see you happy Dee,' I said.

'And it's not nice to see you like this,' she snapped, 'you need to stop thinking of whatever you are thinking...now! Get it out of your head, tell me what it is.'

'I am thinking that a perfect landing is a mirage—the more you chase it, the more it eludes you,' I replied.

'Much like so many other things in life,' she said as she looked away from me and suddenly stopped talking.

'What are you grinning at?' I asked as I turned to look in the direction she was looking at. I saw him get out of his car and walk towards us. By the time my brain could convince my eyes to believe what it was seeing, he had already reached us. 'It is not so difficult to track you girls down, after all,' he said as he hugged Dee.

'What took you so long, Sadu?' Dee asked him as she hugged him back.

'I was in Versova when I got your text, it takes time to drive on these roads,' he answered.

'Hi Meera!' he waved to me airily as I gazed at him with confusion writ large on my face.

'Hi Adi,' I said. 'You texted him?' I asked Dee, narrowing my eyes.

'I was looking for you Em,' he said, 'I thought you were at Aunty's, and when I didn't find you there I had to call Dee.'

I looked at Dee. 'Aditya has something very important to tell you,' she replied earnestly.

'I went to your mother's house looking for you, and this is what I found.' He handed me an envelope.

'What is this?' I asked.

'Open it,' he said. 'You will get something that you have always wanted, and perhaps something that I have always wanted too.'

I saw that it was open on one side; carefully I pulled out its contents. It was my appointment letter as the Commander of the plane that I had flown in the afternoon. I jumped for joy, the letter in my hand, and realized that there was something else in the envelope too. I emptied the contents on to my palm. It was a ring! I looked at Aditya as I absorbed the moment.

'I have been trying to tell you this for the last three days. I could not get engaged to anyone else, because I am too much in love with you, Meera,' he said with a deep sigh. I was smiling but a teardrop still managed to roll down my cheek. He wiped it off with his finger, took me in his arms, and whispered in my ear, 'Will you marry me?'

www.ingramcontent.com/pod-product-compliance
Lightning Source LLC
Chambersburg PA
CBHW020651220526
45464CB00001B/384